THE

SENIOR MOMENTs

Activity Book

THE
SENIOR
MOMENTs
Activity Book

RESTORE YOUR BRAIN TO
ITS TACK-LIKE SHARPNESS!

GEOFF TIBBALLS

Michael O'Mara Books Limited

First published in Great Britain in 2017 by
Michael O'Mara Books Limited
9 Lion Yard
Tremadoc Road
London SW4 7NQ

A CIP catalogue record for this book is available from the British Library.

Papers used by Michael O'Mara Books Limited are natural, recyclable
products made from wood grown in sustainable forests.
The manufacturing processes conform to the environmental
regulations of the country of origin.

ISBN: 978-1-78243-686-7 in paperback

2 3 4 5 6 7 8 9 10

Designed by Design23
Illustrated by Andrew Pinder
Printed and bound by CPI Group (UK) Ltd, Croydon, CRO 4YY
www.mombooks.com

CONTENTS

SECTION 4

SECTION 5

INTRODUCTION

Do you find that your brain power is not what it used to be? Is your IQ battery running low? Do you even struggle to answer the 'either/or' competition questions on daytime TV, do you call your partner 'darling' only because you forgot their real name years ago, and do you get so confused with words that you think a thesaurus became extinct along with the rest of the dinosaurs? Worse still, do you keep having to change your pet's name because you can never remember your online banking password? You now have the only dog in the street that is called 1234.

Thankfully, help is at hand. Experts (where would we be without them?) have devised a series of ideas designed to restore our minds to their tack-like sharpness. They say stress can reduce brain power and they recommend positive thinking as a way of combating it. So from now on, don't tell your partner, 'I think I've lost my car keys.' Think positive. Say, 'I'm sure I've lost my car keys.' They tell us we should stimulate our brain by trying something different, such as learning a musical instrument or taking a new route to work, which is all very well until you have to phone your boss and explain that the reason you are late is because you have been lost in the backstreets for the last two hours or have been trapped overnight in a tuba. Above all, they urge us to make sure we get regular sleep and exercise. Never has there been a better time to take up sleepwalking.

These experts also encourage us to read more books, but not just any book, *this* book. For here you will find a vast range of questions on such diverse subjects as maths, history, science and nature, the arts, food and drink, geography, words and sport that have been hand-picked to test your intellect (or lack of it). Furthermore, each section is tailored to your specific capabilities – whether you feel you still have more faculties than Harvard, or you think you may be starting to lose your marbles, or you fear you may be so far gone that your only future is likely to be an appearance on reality TV. To sum up, there are questions for those who think they know the capital of Andorra, there are questions for those who think they used to own a sweater made of Andorra, and there are questions for those who think they may once have known where Andorra is but can't remember where they put it.

So that you can measure your brain power (or lack of it), all of the answers will be in one place at the back of the book **WHERE YOU CAN FIND THEM.**

SECTION 1

Who knows what they teach kids in schools these days!
But how can anyone be expected to succeed in life
without knowing the valency of zinc or how to solve a
simultaneous equation? Fortunately, you have not only
retained everything you learned in school (you can still
spot an oxbow lake at a hundred paces and remember
the difference between an embankment and a cutting)
but you have also managed to add extra chapters to
your book of knowledge. This may have led to you being
blackballed from your local pub quiz and to your partner
banning all mention at dinner parties of the unusual
migratory habits of the bar-tailed godwit but you feel it
is a small price to pay for becoming the biggest egghead
since Humpty Dumpty. You are convinced that you still
have the brain of a twenty-one-year-old, but sadly not the
body to match. These questions will test how much you
really know and how much is bluster.

HISTORY

1. Whose fate was decided by a Diet of Worms?

   a) John Calvin

   b) Martin Luther

   c) Christopher Robin

2. In medieval France, what was a woman who had committed adultery sometimes required to do by way of punishment?

   a) Have all her teeth extracted in the town square

   b) Stand outside the town hall and dance non-stop for twelve hours while dressed as a badger

   c) Chase a chicken through the streets naked

3. The nursery rhyme 'Ring a Ring o' Roses' refers to which historical event?

   a) The Wars of the Roses

   b) The Black Death

   c) The execution of Marie Antoinette

4. What trait distinguished Queen Mary, consort of King George V of Great Britain?

   a) She was a nymphomaniac

   b) She was a kleptomaniac

   c) She had three funnels

I told you to go easy on the high notes

5. Why was King Charles VI of France terrified of travelling by coach?

a) He was afraid that highwaymen would ambush him and perform unspeakable acts on the royal personage

b) He had a phobia about the rear ends of horses and was scared in case they broke wind in his general direction

c) He was convinced he was made of glass and that the vibration would cause him to shatter into a thousand pieces

6. True or false? The American Civil War got its name because the two sides were extremely polite to each other.

7. In the Defenestration of Prague in 1618, what were people thrown out of?

a) Monasteries

b) Windows

c) Nightclubs

8. Of which American president did H. L. Mencken say: 'If he became convinced tomorrow that coming out for cannibalism would get him the votes he sorely needs, he would begin fattening a missionary in the White House backyard come Wednesday'?

9. What did mad King Otto of Bavaria like to shoot every morning before breakfast?

a) A grouse

b) A pheasant

c) A peasant

10. Whom did the Roman emperor Caligula try to make a consul, to the surprise of many?

a) His mistress

b) His gardener

c) His horse

11. Who ruled England for nine days in 1553? Was it Earl Grey or Lady Jane Grey?

12. What was the nickname of American Civil War commander Thomas Jackson?

a) Longshanks

b) Stonewall

c) Wacko Jacko

13. Which British town was technically at war with Russia for 110 years from the end of the Crimean War until 1966 because of an oversight in the peace treaty?

14. Which one of these kings of England died after falling off the toilet and smashing his head on a cabinet while straining to relieve constipation?

   a) William II
   b) Charles II
   c) George II

15. True or false? Casanova spent the last thirteen years of his life working as a librarian.

16. Sweyn Forkbeard was a feared leader of which army?

   a) The Vikings
   b) The Normans
   c) The Salvation Army

17. **Which wife did Henry VIII uncharitably label 'The Flanders Mare'?**

18. **The severance of which body part belonging to British naval captain Robert Jenkins led to a nine-year war with Spain in the eighteenth century?**

    a) His nose

    b) His ear

    c) His toe

19. **True or false? William the Conqueror's stomach exploded in his coffin.**

20. **What did nineteenth-century British prime minister William Ewart Gladstone take to bed to keep him warm at night?**

    a) The first electric blanket

    b) A hot-water bottle containing tea

    c) Mrs Gladstone

21. **What was the nineteenth-century Princess Alexandra of Bavaria convinced that she had once swallowed as a child?**

    a) A nest of spiders

    b) A toothbrush

    c) A full-sized grand piano

22. **Who described Britain as a 'nation of shopkeepers'?**

    a) Napoleon Bonaparte

    b) Kaiser Wilhelm II

    c) Dorothy Perkins

23. How did Tsar Ivan the Terrible of Russia, the blood-thirsty 'Butcher of Novgorod', die?

a) On the battlefield

b) In a wrestling match with a bear

c) Playing chess

24. True or false? Queen Marie Henriette, wife of Leopold II of the Belgians, kept a pet llama, which she taught to spit in the face of anyone who stroked it.

25. What title did Joshua Abraham Norton, a San Francisco bankrupt, assume in 1859?

a) Head of the San Francisco Chamber of Commerce

b) Mr Universe, 1859

c) Norton I, Emperor of the United States and Protector of Mexico

26. Impressed by stories he had heard about America's new execution method, the electric chair, Emperor Menelik II of Abyssinia ordered three such chairs for his country. What stopped him putting them to effective use?

a) Nobody in Abyssinia committed a crime punishable by death

b) The imperial guards refused to carry out executions

c) Abyssinia did not yet have electricity

Answers on page 211

SCIENCE AND NATURE

1. **To deter predators, what is the caterpillar of the king page swallowtail butterfly disguised as?**

   a) A snake's head

   b) Bird droppings

   c) Vladimir Putin

2. **A German Shepherd dog was arrested in the Spanish city of Seville for doing what?**

   a) Persistently fouling the pavement

   b) Snatching handbags from shoppers

   c) Biting the mayor on his backside

3. **True or false? A newly discovered species of praying mantis has been named after Lindsay Lohan.**

4. **What part of the human body is the philtrum?**

   a) The groove between the base of your nose and your upper lip

   b) The piece of skin at the back of your ear lobe

   c) The area of the brain that helps you to remember people's names ... or not

5. Arctic, red and fennec are types of which animal?

   a) Fox

   b) Hare

   c) Deer

6. Mammatus, cirrostratus and altocumulus are all types of what?

7. To what position on Japan's Kishigawa railway line was Tama the cat appointed in 2007?

   a) Ticket collector

   b) Stationmaster

   c) Station announcer

8. Individual bulbs of which flower often changed hands for hundreds of pounds in the 1630s?

   a) Crocus

   b) Tulip

   c) Daffodil

9. Why did silent-movie star Clara Bow dye the fur of her pet Chow dogs red?

   a) She was an ardent Communist

   b) To match the colour of her own hair

   c) She couldn't stand the sight of blood on her dogs

10. True or false? Dobermans take their name from a nineteenth-century German tax collector, Ludwig Dobermann, who bred the dogs to help him put the frighteners on clients.

11. When George's wife tells him that he has the memory of a goldfish, what figure ought she to have in mind, according to recent research?

a) Three seconds

b) Three minutes

c) Three months

12. What type of creature is a tasselled wobbegong?

a) Spider

b) Monkey

c) Shark

13. The name of what animal can precede frog, finch and dog?

14. What breed of bird used to be taken down coal mines to detect the presence of any dangerous gases?

a) Mynah bird

b) Canary

c) Ostrich

15. Which of these became extinct in 1914, having once been the most abundant bird in North America with a population of up to five billion?

a) Traveller pigeon

b) Commuter pigeon

c) Passenger pigeon

16. Before all-porcelain false teeth were perfected in the nineteenth century, what were dentures often made from?

a) The teeth of dead dogs

b) Old piano keys

c) The teeth pulled from soldiers who had been killed in battle

17. True or false? Abu Dhabi stages an annual beauty contest for camels.

18. Which of these was once considered an effective method for curing a child of whooping cough?

a) Passing the child three times under the belly of a donkey

b) Standing the child on its head for two hours

c) Feeding the child a medicine of nettle juice and dog drool

19. Carpet, gaboon and hognose are all types of which species of snake?

20. According to a survey, what did one-third of dog owners in the United States admit doing to their pets?

a) Teaching them to use Windows 10

b) Teaching them to speak Cat

c) Leaving messages for them on answering machines

21. True or false? In 1949, a flock of starlings landed on the minute hand of Big Ben, slowing it down by five minutes.

22. Which of these is a nocturnal mammal from Madagascar?

a) Pee-pee

b) Aye-aye

c) Oh-oh

23. What fastening device was invented by Georges de Mestral?

a) Rubber band

b) Velcro

c) Zip

24. What is designed by Christian Louboutin, Manolo Blahnik and Jimmy Choo?

a) Shoes

b) Hats

c) Toupees

25. Harpy, Bonelli's and Wedge-tailed are all species of which bird?

a) Warbler

b) Eagle

c) Thrush

26. Which personal hygiene aid was invented by American scientist Dr Buddy Lapidus in 1975?

a) Roll-on deodorant

b) Soap on a rope

c) Odor-Eaters

Answers on page 211

MATHS

1. George phoned an insurance company call centre at 10.04 a.m. and thirty-five minutes later he was still waiting in a queue while an automated voice on the other end told him how important his call was to them. His favourite TV programme starts at 10.50 a.m., so, given that it takes him two minutes to get downstairs and settled in front of the TV, how long will it be before George slams down the phone and tells the insurance company where it can stick its special premium for valued customers?

2. How many is threescore and ten?

3. On 23 March George faithfully promised his wife that he would replace the bolt on the bathroom door. First, he mislaid his screwdriver, then the screws and, lastly, the new bolt, with the result that he finally fitted it on 19 May. How many days did his wife have to wait for him to complete a job, which, as she so eloquently put it, 'a trained monkey could have done in fifteen minutes'?

4. True or false? Gross ignorance is 144 times worse than ordinary ignorance.

5. George has eight pairs of identical, matching black socks, but every two weeks one sock mysteriously disappears, never to be seen again. Assuming that he is too mean to buy replacements, how many weeks will it be until he no longer has a pair of socks?

6. Algebra: If A=2 and B=3, how much were ABBA worth?

7. Sylvia spends six hours a day with her head in a puzzle book and two hours a day doing housework. Expressed as a ratio, what greater importance does Sylvia attach to doing word searches than she does to keeping the house clean?

8. George's wife is serving ten potatoes for four people, including herself. George insists on having twice as many as everybody else, so how many potatoes is he served?

9. If you had three address books containing forty-three, fifty-one and twenty-seven names respectively – and none were duplicated – how many addresses would you have in total?

10. George can climb eight steps in one minute, so how many minutes would it take him to climb the 1,576 steps of the Empire State Building – and because paramedics can climb seventy-two steps in one minute, how long would it take them to the nearest minute to reach him at the top and administer much-needed oxygen?

11. Without using a calculator, what is the square root of 121?

12. George has planted six delphiniums in his garden. Each plant attracts three hungry slugs per night. Over the course of two weeks, how many of the slimy little devils must George butcher in order to preserve his precious delphiniums?

Answers on page 211

THE ARTS

1. Which duo were not allowed to touch on 1960s' British television?

a) Sonny and Cher

b) Sooty and Soo

c) Lyndon and Lady Bird Johnson

2. Phil 'Philthy Animal' Taylor was a member of which band?

a) Black Sabbath

b) Motörhead

c) Brotherhood of Man

3. Which author wrote *Jurassic Park*, *Disclosure* and *Prey*?

4. What does the 'T' stand for in the name of *Star Trek* captain James T. Kirk?

a) Trevor

b) Tarquin

c) Tiberius

5. True or false? In his seventies, distinguished actor Sir Ralph Richardson used to ride around London on a motorcycle with his pet parrot tucked inside his jacket.

6. Pink Floyd's first hit 'Arnold Layne' was about a man who collected what?

a) Butterflies

b) Stamps

c) Ladies' underwear

7. What was unusual about the exhibition of Henri Matisse's nautical painting *Le Bateau* at New York's Museum of Modern Art in 1961?

a) A careless gallery worker put his elbow through the canvas

b) The tide in the painting started to come in on the second day

c) It was accidentally hung upside down for over a month without anybody noticing

8. What words did Paul McCartney originally use instead of 'yesterday' while composing the lyrics for the song of that title?

a) Scrambled eggs

b) Elbow pads

c) Monkey nuts

9. In the 1980 movie *Airplane!*, what is the reply of Dr Rumack (Leslie Nielsen) when Ted Striker (Robert Hays) says: 'Surely you can't be serious'?

10. Who sang about 'Cathy's Clown'?

a) The Everly Brothers

b) The Righteous Brothers

c) The Chuckle Brothers

11. Which of these was a character in *Happy Days*?

a) Chuck Muck

b) Harry Parry

c) Ralph Malph

12. *Gone with the Wind* **is which author's only novel?**

13. What did Beethoven do to stimulate his brain while composing?

a) Climbed to the summit of a hill near his home

b) Dipped his head in a bowl of iced water

c) Watched episodes of *The Real Housewives of Beverly Hills*

14. What is the name of fictional Belgian detective Hercule Poirot's secretary?

a) Miss Lime

b) Miss Lemon

c) Miss Satsuma

15. What is ironic about rock band ZZ Top's Frank Beard?

16. Where did legendary French actress Sarah Bernhardt like to learn her lines?

a) In the bath

b) In a coffin

c) In a state of undress

17. True or false? The Beatles were once the support act to Lenny the Lion.

18. Hamilton Burger was the adversary of which character?

a) Ronald McDonald

b) Columbo

c) Perry Mason

19. Where or what was Gene Pitney twenty-four hours from in 1963?

a) Toledo

b) Tulsa

c) Meltdown

20. Which character in a Washington Irving short story slept for twenty years?

21. Which 1970s movie carried the tagline 'Hell, Upside Down'?

a) *The Towering Inferno*

b) *The Poseidon Adventure*

c) *Saturday Night Fever*

22. True or false? Ernest Hemingway made a decorative table ornament out of his own earwax.

23. Under what name did Simon and Garfunkel perform in their early days?

a) Tom and Jerry

b) Pixie and Dixie

c) Yogi Bear and Boo Boo

24. Which film star was once banned in Romania because the authorities thought he would scare small children?

a) Charlie Chaplin

b) Oliver Hardy

c) Mickey Mouse

25. What is the name of Spider-Man's alter ego?

26. **Before she was famous, what did American singer Cyndi Lauper used to clean for a living?**

   a) Toilets

   b) Bus depots

   c) Dog kennels

27. **True or false? Ian Anderson, the singer with Jethro Tull, sometimes used to walk around wearing a lampshade on his head.**

28. **Which artist is famous for his paintings of water lilies?**

   a) Monet

   b) Manet

   c) Millais

29. **Which UK rock band started out as the High Numbers?**

30. **Which author created the character Jack Reacher?**

   a) P. D. James

   b) Val McDermid

   c) Lee Child

31. **'I am a weakish speller' is an anagram of which famous playwright's name?**

32. **What type of cowboy did Glen Campbell sing about in 1975?**

   a) Lonesome

   b) Rhinestone

   c) Nine-stone

33. **What is Red Hot Chili Peppers guitarist Michael Balzary better known as?**

34. **Of which US rock 'n' roller did Rolling Stone Keith Richards say: 'I couldn't warm to him even if I was cremated next to him'?**

   a) Jerry Lee Lewis

   b) Chuck Berry

   c) The Big Bopper

Answers on page 211

FOOD AND DRINK

1. What is the chief ingredient of the Inuit dish *kiviak*?

   a) Walrus flipper

   b) Auk

   c) Seal

2. The consumption of which banned drink was liable to result in execution in seventeenth-century Turkey?

   a) Beer

   b) Wine

   c) Coffee

3. True or false? In the United States, you are four times more likely to be killed by a vending machine than a shark.

4. In 1937, what became the first frozen food to go on sale in Britain?

   a) Green beans

   b) Garden peas

   c) Asparagus

5. From which country does Leffe beer originate?

6. Which of these is an alternative name for the fish more commonly known as hake?

a) Keith

b) Colin

c) Graham

7. Rocky Mountain Oysters are another name for which dubious North American delicacy?

a) Rattlesnake's eyeballs

b) Elk's ears

c) Bull's testicles

8. True or false? Cooks in the Outer Hebrides make a nice *jus* with the liquid squeezed from the intestines of a dead gannet.

9. Which of these is a variety of apple?

a) Fecking Farmer

b) Bloody Ploughman

c) Damned Drayman

10. What does 'pumpernickel' – a sweet rye bread – translate into in German?

a) Devil's fart

b) Wolf's foot

c) Witch's hood

11. If a Maris Piper was placed in front of you, would you try to get a tune out of it or mash it?

12. What colour Smartie was ousted from British tubes in 1989 to make way for the new blue Smartie that had proved popular in other parts of Europe?

a) Light brown

b) Green

c) Pink

13. What was the name of the world's first self-service grocery store, which opened in Memphis, Tennessee, in 1916?

a) Higgledy Piggledy

b) Piggly Wiggly

c) Willy Wonka

14. True or false? The durian fruit of south-east Asia smells so foul that passengers are banned from taking it on most public transport systems.

15. If you ate *cuy* in Peru, what would you be putting in your mouth?

a) Hamster

b) Guinea pig

c) Cat

16. Lollo rosso, Batavia and Little Gem are all varieties of which vegetable?

17. Which of these is the name of a Swedish chocolate bar?

a) Plopp

b) Poop

c) Crapp

18. What is Cornish Yarg cheese covered in?

a) Anchovies

b) Nettles

c) Dead flies

19. *Smalahove* – a complete sheep's head (including eyes, lips and ears) – is a traditional dish in which country?

a) Bulgaria

b) Norway

c) Latvia

20. **From where did mayonnaise originate?**

a) Mahon, Menorca

b) Mayenne, France

c) County Mayo, Ireland

21. **Which spice comes from the flower of the crocus?**

a) Cinnamon

b) Saffron

c) Tamarind

22. **If you ordered calamari in a restaurant, what would you be eating?**

a) Crayfish

b) Mussels

c) Squid

23. **What is the Welsh product laverbread made from?**

a) Seaweed

b) Grass

c) Rabbit droppings

24. **Who said: 'I will not eat oysters. I want my food dead. Not sick. Not wounded. Dead'?**

a) Oscar Wilde

b) Dwight D. Eisenhower

c) Woody Allen

Answers on page 212

SPORT

1. Which sport's world championships are staged annually at Fenny Bentley in Derbyshire?

a) Shin kicking

b) Gnat swatting

c) Toe wrestling

2. Which American golfer was once described by commentator David Feherty as having 'a swing like a man trying to kill a snake in a phone booth'?

a) Bubba Watson

b) Tom Kite

c) Jim Furyk

3. Wrigley Field is a baseball stadium in which American city?

4. True or false? Competing in the 1979 European Figure Skating Championships, Jayne Torvill and Christopher Dean received perfect scores of 6.0 (apart from a 5.8 from the East German judge) despite falling through the ice at one point in their routine.

5. The Swaythling Cup is associated with which sport?

a) Lacrosse

b) Table tennis

c) Tiddlywinks

6. What did Finnish Formula One driver Kimi Raikkonen apparently dress up as to avoid identification during a motorboat race in 2007?

a) Batman

b) A gorilla

c) Bette Midler

7. If you were in the 'egg position', in which sport would you be taking part?

a) Kiteboarding

b) Cricket

c) Downhill skiing

8. The number 111 in cricket is known by what name?

a) Nelson

b) Wellington

c) Napoleon

9. Which Italian world heavyweight boxing champion of the 1930s was nicknamed 'The Ambling Alp' because he was 6 feet, 6 inches tall?

10. What is unusual about Australia's Henley-on-Todd boat race?

a) The rowers wear suits of armour

b) The boats are made of beer cans

c) The riverbed is dry

11. True or false? Most competitors in the ancient Olympic Games ran or wrestled in the nude.

12. Which Brazilian footballer was nicknamed 'Little Bird'?

a) Rivaldo

b) Garrincha

c) Ronaldo

13. What happened at the 1979 Pan-American Games to Wallace Williams, a marathon runner representing the Virgin Islands?

a) He was chased off course for three miles by a pack of wild dogs

b) He was accidentally run over by the camera car that was filming the race

c) He was so slow that by the time he reached the stadium, it was locked and everyone had gone home

14. Of which fellow boxer did Muhammad Ali say: 'He's so ugly that when he cries the tears run down the back of his head'?

15. Why was the American team late arriving in Greece for the 1896 Olympic Games?

a) They had forgotten their running shoes and had to turn back

b) Their ship capsized off the coast of Portugal

c) They were using the wrong calendar

16. A special race featuring which animals was staged at Romford Greyhound Stadium in 1937?

a) Donkeys

b) Cheetahs

c) Tortoises

17. Meadowlark Lemon was a flamboyant star player at which sport?

18. Which Canadian snooker player once drank seventy-six cans of lager during a match in Australia?

   a) Cliff Thorburn

   b) Bill Werbeniuk

   c) Kirk Stevens

19. Whose world long jump record achieved at the 1968 Mexico Olympics stood for almost twenty-three years until it was broken by Mike Powell in 1991?

20. What did Swiss-Portuguese footballer Paulo Diogo leave behind on the perimeter fence after scoring in a 2004 Swiss League game?

   a) A boot

   b) His shorts

   c) Part of his finger

21. At which sport – other than angling – might you 'catch a crab'?

   a) Badminton

   b) Judo

   c) Rowing

22. True or false? American jockey Frank Hayes was found dead in the saddle after riding 20-1 outsider Sweet Kiss to victory in a steeplechase at Belmont Park in 1923.

23. What is the name of the Major League baseball team from St Louis?

a) Cardinals

b) Bishops

c) Deacons

24. Why was the 1887 world middleweight boxing title fight between Jack 'Nonpareil' Dempsey and Johnny Reagan on Long Island, New York, abandoned after eight rounds?

a) Both boxers collapsed with exhaustion

b) The tide came in and flooded the ring

c) The referee had to leave to collect his daughter from kindergarten

25. Young Boys and Grasshoppers are the names of professional football teams in which country?

26. Jay Silverheels, who played Tonto in the TV series *The Lone Ranger*, was a professional at which sport?

a) Lacrosse

b) Ice hockey

c) Show jumping

27. What make of car did Jim Clark drive to become Formula One World Champion in 1963 and 1965?

a) BRM

b) Lotus

c) Reliant Robin

28. The Denver Broncos, the Oakland Raiders and the Washington Redskins all play which sport?

29. Which one of these statements is true?

a) Australian Test cricketer 'Chuck' Fleetwood-Smith used to liven up a dull game by performing bird impressions as he came in to bowl

b) Former England soccer international Wilf Mannion used to drop his shorts every time he took a corner

c) Former world heavyweight boxing champion Sonny Liston used to chew razor blades before a big fight

30. Which West Indies fast bowler of the 1970s and 1980s was known as 'Whispering Death'?

31. 'Dump', 'Wipe' and 'Floater' are terms used in which sport?

a) Table Tennis

b) Volleyball

c) Squash

Answers on page 212

GEOGRAPHY

1. In which county does the River Thames rise?

a) Oxfordshire

b) Gloucestershire

c) Donegal

2. A Hoosier is a native of which American state?

3. Where would you find Table Mountain?

a) Cape Town

b) Rio de Janeiro

c) IKEA winter sale

4. True or false? The highest point in the Maldives is less than eight feet above sea level.

5. Which sea is located off the east coast of Canada?

a) Setter Sea

b) Beagle Sea

c) Labrador Sea

6. How do members of the Masai tribe of Tanzania and Kenya traditionally greet each other on religious holidays?

a) By putting each other in a headlock

b) By kissing each other's big toe

c) By spitting on each other

7. What are the eight American states whose names begin and end with a vowel?

8. Which South Pacific island is home to more than a thousand mysterious giant statues?

a) Easter Island

b) Christmas Island

c) Shrove Tuesday Island

9. What is the capital of Azerbaijan?

a) Baku

b) Bakup

c) Bakov

10. True or false? The mayor of the Turkish city of Batman threatened to sue Warner Bros. for using its name in the title of the superhero movie *Batman Begins*.

11. The Apennines are a mountain range in which country?

12. What is celebrated globally on 23 February each year?

a) International Take a Tarantula to the Office Day

b) International Dog Biscuit Appreciation Day

c) International Trim Your Toenails Day

13. True or false? Bird droppings are the chief export of the Pacific island of Nauru.

14. Where would you find Disko Island?

a) In the Mediterranean Sea

b) Off the coast of Greenland

c) Off the coast of San Francisco

15. What is the national currency of Bulgaria?

a) Lek

b) Lev

c) Dong

16. In 1973, British Honduras was officially renamed as which country?

17. Phillip Island is located off which country?

a) Argentina

b) South Africa

c) Australia

18. Why do many churches in Malta have two clocks showing different times?

a) They have never quite got the hang of Maltese Summer Time

b) It is the result of an old dispute between two local timekeepers

c) To confuse Satan about the time of the next service

19. What does Khartoum, the capital city of Sudan, translate into in English?

a) Camel's hump

b) Vulture's wing

c) Elephant's trunk

20. Nineteenth-century travel pioneer Thomas Cook was secretary of which organization?

a) Leicester Rodent Exterminators' Society

b) Leicester Temperance Society

c) Leicester Club 1830

21. What is the state capital of Montana?

a) Hannah

b) Helena

c) Billings

22. True or false? Any person granted the freedom of the Welsh city of Cardiff has the right to run naked around the castle walls on two specified dates in the calendar year.

23. Which of these is not the name of a genuine museum?

a) Moist Towelette Museum

b) Burnt Food Museum

c) International Cotton Bud Museum

24. London, Cambridge, Peterborough, Stratford and Windsor are all cities in which Canadian province?

25. Which country owns the Atlantic island of Madeira?

a) Spain

b) Portugal

c) France

26. Which American city is home to the Liberty Bell?

a) Philadelphia

b) Buffalo

c) New Orleans

27. Which three South American countries does the equator pass through?

28. Which two of these are not Caribbean islands?

a) Guadeloupe

b) Saint Kitts and Nevis

c) Martinique

d) Mauritius

e) Montserrat

f) Sint Maarten

g) Nicobar

h) Turks and Caicos Islands

29. What does Mamungkukumpurangkuntjunya Hill – Australia's longest official place name – translate as?

a) Where the koala resides

b) Where the devil urinates

c) Where the beers are always cold

Answers on page 212

WORDS

1. **What is turophobia a fear of?**

   a) Clowns

   b) Cheese

   c) Stick insects

2. **What is the name for the dot over a lower-case 'i' or 'j'?**

   a) Wattle

   b) Mottle

   c) Tittle

3. **True or false? The phrase 'hair of the dog' originates from the medieval belief that the best way to treat a bite from a rabid dog was to place a hair from the same dog across the wound.**

4. **George is prone to the occasional thorough cough. Does this mean that he?**

   a) Coughs and breaks wind at the same time

   b) Coughs so violently that his dentures fall out

   c) Coughs while he is eating, thereby spraying morsels far and wide

5. **What word links cauliflower and lobe?**

6. Someone who is described as 'struthious' might be said to resemble which creature?

a) A snake

b) A fox

c) An ostrich

7. If you suffer from narcolepsy, do you struggle to?

a) Fall asleep

b) Stay awake

c) Control your temper

8. What word can precede moon, suckle and badger?

9. George's wife has been overdosing on crosswords and one day tells him that he is being 'contumacious'. Is she accusing him of being ... ?

a) Overly aggressive

b) Wilfully disobedient

c) Excessively lazy

10. What is the name for the collective noun of a group of crows?

a) Homicide

b) Assassination

c) Murder

How come we get such a bad press?

11. What important word translates as *pivo* in Czech, *øl* in Danish and *cerveza* in Spanish?

12. Where did George's wife find to be the ideal place for a kirby grip?

a) On her shoe

b) In her hair

c) On George's tongue

13. What is a snollygoster?

a) An unexpectedly powerful sneeze

b) An unscrupulous politician

c) An extremely sexy woman

14. What word links bar, milk and pigeon?

15. What would you do with a nasturtium?

a) Plant it

b) Blow into it

c) Ride it

16. Is an oxter the name for a hipster ox or an old English term for an armpit?

17. If you bumfuzzle someone, do you?

a) Chastise them

b) Stroke them

c) Confuse them

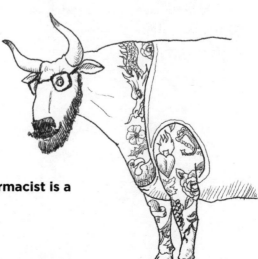

18. True or false? A pharmacist is a helper on a farm.

19. If you were parsimonious, would you be?

a) Deeply religious

b) Mean with money

c) Fond of parsley

20. When Sylvia's brother wrote down his birthday list and said he wanted a board for mixing paints, why were his family mystified to see he had requested a new palate?

21. What word can precede broker, car and room?

22. Which of these is a Victorian word for fondling and generally being amorous?

a) Crungescrunching

b) Bamdiddling

c) Firkytoodling

23. What word describes someone who repairs shoes and a popular North American fruit pie, often made with blueberries?

24. *Pamplemousse* is the French word for which fruit?

a) Pineapple

b) Raspberry

c) Grapefruit

25. What is anatidaephobia a fear of?

a) Suffocating in blancmange

b) Being sucked down the plughole while taking a bath

c) Being watched by a duck

Answers on page 213

SECTION 2

Although you struggle to get your head around the fact that Nyasaland doesn't exist anymore and you would still rather embrace a grizzly bear than the metric system, you feel confident that your intellect is pretty sharp for someone of your age – and you don't mind putting it to the test. For you, Sudoku is the new rock 'n' roll. It's only your short-term memory that lets you down sometimes. For example, you can name every member of *The Magnificent Seven* but have no idea why you just went into the tool shed. It could be something to do with a screwdriver but you can't be sure. The reason will, of course, come back to you – usually at about three o'clock in the morning. In the meantime, see if any of these questions keep you awake at night.

HISTORY

1. In 1927, which American aviator made the first transatlantic flight?

   a) Orville Wright

   b) Charles Lindbergh

   c) Dick Dastardly

2. On which ship did the Pilgrim Fathers sail to America?

   a) *Golden Hind*

   b) *Mayflower*

   c) *Titanic*

3. Which confused King of England is said to have shaken hands with the branches of an oak tree in Windsor Great Park and talked to it for several minutes in the belief that it was the King of Prussia?

4. Who once said: 'Trying is the first step towards failure?'

a) Franklin D. Roosevelt

b) Ronald Reagan

c) Homer Simpson

5. What did Holy Roman Emperor Charles V sack in 1527?

a) His hairdresser

b) His manservant

c) Rome

6. True or false? Catherine the Great of Russia was so angry when she found dandruff on her collar that she imprisoned her hairdresser in an iron cage for three years.

7. What did Peter the Great of Russia insist should be kept in a jar of alcohol on his wife's bedside table?

a) His false teeth

b) Her favourite pet dog

c) The severed head of her lover

8. Who finished as runners-up to the Roundheads in the English Civil Wars of 1642 to 1651?

9. What was the name of the botched invasion of Cuba in 1961 by a CIA-sponsored paramilitary group that heightened world tension?

a) Bay of Pigs

b) Bay of Swine

c) Bay of Sheep

10. Louis XIV of France reportedly owned more than 1,000 what?

a) Tape measures

b) Wigs

c) Mistresses

11. Which famous Frenchman was described by Winston Churchill as looking 'like a female llama who has just been surprised in her bath'?

a) Charles de Gaulle

b) Georges Pompidou

c) Arsène Wenger

12. In which century was the Battle of Bannockburn?

13. Which of these were famous nineteenth-century Australian explorers?

a) Burke and Wills

b) Burke and Hare

c) Burke and Head

14. The Great Fire of London in 1666 started in a bakery located on which street?

a) Bread Lane

b) Pudding Lane

c) Cycle Lane

15. True or false? King Haakon VII of Norway died in 1957 after slipping on the soap in his marble bath and hitting his head on the taps.

16. When the Turks ran out of ammunition at the Battle of Lepanto in 1571, what did they hurl at Austrian soldiers?

a) Oranges and lemons

b) Sticks and stones

c) Sarcasm

17. Which weaving device was invented by James Hargreaves in the early years of the Industrial Revolution?

a) Spinning Jenny

b) Spinning Jilly

c) Puffing Billy

18. What did the Marquis de Sade's mother become?

a) A dentist

b) A tax official

c) A nun

19. The repeated failure of which crop resulted in a nineteenth-century famine in Ireland?

a) Potato

b) Cabbage

c) Mangetout

20. Who was the second president of the United States?

21. Who captained the _Endeavour,_ the first European ship to reach the east coast of Australia?

a) Captain Morgan

b) Captain Cook

c) Captain Birdseye

d) Captain and Tennille

22. Oswald Mosley was the leader of which twentieth-century fascist group?

a) Blackshirts

b) Sweatshirts

c) Nightshirts

23. Which section of society did Pope Urban VIII threaten to excommunicate in 1642?

a) Snuff users

b) Dog owners

c) Second-hand cart salesmen

24. True or false? King Edward VI of England was not allowed to rule unaided because he was a miner?

25. Which Italian statesman gave his name to a type of biscuit?

a) Mussolini

b) Berlusconi

c) Garibaldi

26. What did early Victorian rail passengers fear would happen to them if they travelled at speeds in excess of 50mph?

a) Their heads would blow off

b) The ticket collector would be violently ill over them

c) The buffet trolley would veer dangerously out of control

27. Who once said: 'If I had to live my life over again, I'd be a plumber'?

a) John Lennon

b) Albert Einstein

c) Liberace

Well, don't say I didn't warn you ...

28. Who was the first person to sail around the world?

29. Ypres, the Somme and Passchendaele were battles in which war?

a) World War I

b) World War II

c) The Hundred Years' War

30. Morton's fork was a device implemented by King Henry VII of England for doing what?

a) Cooking crumpets

b) Relieving constipation

c) Collecting taxes

31. In which city did an infamous 'Tea Party' take place in 1773?

a) Washington

b) Boston

c) Tunbridge Wells

32. Where was Jean-Paul Marat, one of the leaders of the French Revolution, murdered?

a) In his bed

b) In his bath

c) In his local bistro

33. True or false? Queen Ranavalona I of Madagascar ordered the execution of any of her subjects who appeared in her dreams.

34. Who wrote the *Odyssey*?

a) Ovid

b) Homer

c) Bart

35. What adjective was bestowed on *Titanic* survivor Molly Brown?

a) Unsinkable

b) Unfashionable

c) Insatiable

36. What was the first name of the nineteenth-century Prussian statesman von Bismarck?

a) Klaus

b) Otto

c) Nigel

37. True or false? Louis XIX was King of France for just twenty minutes before abdicating in favour of his nephew.

38. Which of these is *not* a fictional character?

a) Ming the Merciless

b) Vlad the Impaler

c) Conan the Barbarian

Answers on page 213

SCIENCE AND NATURE

1. A waxing gibbous is a type of?

a) Bird

b) Moon

c) Monkey

2. True or false? The flamingo always feeds with its beak upside down.

3. What can a mudskipper do that most other fish can't?

a) Swim backwards

b) Move around on dry land

c) Play the ukulele

4. Christopher Cockerell invented which mode of transport?

a) Hovercraft

b) Segway

c) Stilts

5. Elephant, water and pygmy are all types of which mammal?

a) Giraffe

b) Shrew

c) Otter

6. What plant with purple or white flowers is also said to be the best policy?

7. When did T. rex become extinct?

a) 45 million years ago

b) 65 million years ago

c) 1977, when Marc Bolan died

8. What animal lives in a lodge?

a) Squirrel

b) Beaver

c) Freemason

9. True or false? When the first duck-billed platypus was taken to Europe, scientists were convinced that it was not a real animal and tried to pull its beak off.

10. According to popular legend, what fell from a tree and hit Isaac Newton on the head to inspire him to develop his theory of gravity?

a) An apple

b) A pineapple

c) A cow

11. What is the claim to fame of the desert rat?

a) It can smell other desert rats from up to 100 miles away

b) It mates more than 120 times in an hour

c) It is the only rodent to win the Nobel Prize for Literature

12. As well as being something that George used to experience in his younger days, what else is 'morning glory'?

13. Which of these is a type of dinosaur?

a) Velocipede

b) Velociraptor

c) Velodrome

14. What birds are said to bring bad luck should they ever leave the Tower of London?

a) Ravens

b) Pigeons

c) Penguins

15. True or false? Every Zimbabwean supermarket has a real zebra on standby at the checkouts in case any items are missing a barcode.

16. The basenji hunting dog from Africa is unable to bark, but makes what type of sound instead?

a) Whistle

b) Yodel

c) Laugh

17. What did the UK Meteorological Office start doing to storms in 2016?

a) Sending them threatening letters

b) Putting up diversion signs in the direction of France

c) Naming them

18. The cheetah is the only big cat that cannot do what?

a) Purr

b) Fully retract its claws

c) Ride a bicycle

19. According to studies, what do women do almost twice as much as men?

a) Sneeze

b) Blink

c) Hog the TV remote

20. What freshwater fish shares its name with something that a bird sits on?

21. **The rock hyrax, a small, furry rodent found in the Middle East, is the closest living relative of which animal?**

   a) Anteater

   b) Sealion

   c) Elephant

22. **The poisonous plant deadly nightshade belongs to the same family as which edible food?**

   a) Cabbage

   b) Potato

   c) Strawberry

23. **True or false? Bluetooth technology is named after tenth-century Viking king Harald Bluetooth who promoted unity between Denmark and Norway.**

24. **Where was Archimedes sitting when he had his 'Eureka!' moment?**

   a) In his favourite chair

   b) In the bath

   c) On Mrs Archimedes' lap

25. **Which of these is not a species of sea bird?**

   a) Noddy

   b) Gobby

   c) Booby

Answers on page 213

MATHS

1. **George has a box of 120 golf balls. He plays twice a week and loses an average of four balls per round. How many weeks will it be until George runs out of balls and finally admits he can't play the game?**

2. Sylvia is a bit-part actress who once appeared alongside Al Pacino – in the queue for the catering van on location. Her birthday is 7 February, but her online biography states that she has been fifty-nine since 2008. What birthday did Sylvia really celebrate on 7 February 2017?

3. **On average, George loses his car keys once every two weeks. So how many times over the last two years has he asked his wife accusingly: 'Have you seen my car keys?'**

4. If it takes one workman one hour to dig a hole, how long will it take three workmen to dig the same hole (excluding tea breaks)?

5. **George receives an average of forty cold calls a month from injury lawyers and each one lasts fifteen seconds before George slams the phone down. In the course of a year, how many minutes of his time is wasted listening to salespeople trying to convince him that he has had an accident that wasn't his fault?**

6. On holiday in Spain, Sylvia insisted that her husband hire a taxi from the hotel to the local bar because it was 'two miles away' and much too far to walk. The actual distance was 500 yards. By how many yards was Sylvia exaggerating and why wasn't her husband in the least bit surprised?

7. **Unbeknown to his wife, George had a nice win on a horse, so he secretly arranged to meet his pals Alec and Eric for a celebratory drink in a bar. Earlier in the day, George's wife had told him that dinner would be served at home at 7 p.m. precisely. George arrived at the bar at 5.50, but lost track of the time and didn't leave until 7.35. It was then a fifteen-minute walk to his home. How late was George for dinner, and might he be advised to buy an expensive present for his wife with his winnings before confessing about his gambling?**

8. If your new TV has 101 channels but eighty-nine are of no interest whatsoever, how many channels are actually worth watching occasionally?

9. **George's three teenage granddaughters came to stay in readiness for a family meal at a local restaurant. Before going out to dinner, each girl took it in turns to use the bathroom. Louisa, the eldest, spent one hour and twenty minutes in the bathroom taking a shower and sorting out her hair extensions. Then Emily, the middle one, spent fifty-five minutes in the bathroom taking a shower and manicuring her nails. Finally Kate, the youngest, spent fifty minutes in the bathroom taking a shower and moisturizing her skin. For how long was George effectively barred from the bathroom with his legs crossed?**

10. A ladder hangs over the side of a ship so that the bottom rung rests on the surface of the water. The rungs are one foot apart and as the tide comes in the water rises at a rate of four inches per hour. How long will it be until three rungs are covered?

11. **George is having one of his senior moments. He remembers putting his passport in a drawer, but he can't remember which one. There are eight possible drawers and it takes him three minutes to look through each one. How long will he spend searching for his passport before he remembers that it is in his coat pocket?**

12. How many eggs are there in seven dozen?

13. **George went fishing. In the course of the day, he caught an old tyre, a training shoe, a car bumper, a small fish and a Michael Bolton CD. What fraction of the items for which he spent nine hours on the riverbank sitting in the cold and pouring rain were destined for the dinner table?**

14. Sylvia persuades her husband to help her choose a new pair of shoes. On average, she spends ten minutes in each shop and there is then a five-minute walk to the next one. After three hours how many shoe shops has she visited before deciding that the pair she really liked was in the very first shop they went to?

15. **George has been married for forty years, but for the last eight years he has completely forgotten his wedding anniversary. What percentage of his married life has he remembered his anniversary and, unless his memory improves dramatically, on a scale of one to ten what are his chances of reaching forty-one years of marriage?**

Answers on page 214

THE ARTS

1. Which rock drummer's real name is Christopher Millar?

a) Ringo Starr

b) Animal

c) Rat Scabies

2. What was the profession of the Crane brothers in the TV series *Frasier*?

a) Bricklayer

b) Professional boxer

c) Psychiatrist

3. To which great writer and thinker is attributed the quote 'I have nothing to declare but my genius'?

a) Karl Marx

b) Oscar Wilde

c) George W. Bush

4. What unusual job did Sylvester Stallone have before making it as an actor?

a) Rat-catcher

b) Goldfish trainer

c) Lion cage cleaner

5. Which long-running American TV series was based on a novel by Grace Metalious?

a) *M*A*S*H*

b) *Peyton Place*

c) *The Flying Nun*

6. True or false? Eric Clapton took his stage name from the area of London to which he and his family moved when he was twelve. His real name is Eric Ponders End.

7. Squirrel Nutkin is a character in books by which author?

a) Enid Blyton

b) Beatrix Potter

c) Stephen King

8. In what garment was horror film star Bela Lugosi buried?

a) Dracula's cloak

b) A Green Bay Packers jersey

c) A pink tutu

9. Who composed 'The Clock' Symphony?

a) Joseph Haydn

b) Frédéric Chopin

c) Russ Conway

10. Which English actress played Agatha Christie's Miss Marple on TV from 1984 to 1992?

11. Which of these was the title of a Prince song?

    a) 'Little Red Cadillac'

    b) 'Little Red Corvette'

    c) 'Little Red Rooster'

12. What was the name of the International Man of Mystery played by Mike Myers in a 1997 movie?

    a) Austin Powers

    b) Clark Kent

    c) Kim Jong-il

13. According to the title of his 1969 hit, what was American singer Tommy Roe feeling?

    a) Lousy

    b) Sleepy

    c) Dizzy

14. What make of car was Herbie, star of the movie *The Love Bug*?

15. According to a TV commercial of the 1950s, 'you'll wonder where the yellow went when you brush your teeth with ...' what?

    a) Gibbs SR

    b) Pepsodent

    c) Tar

16. Which of these was not a member of Top Cat's gang?

    a) Benny the Ball

    b) Brain

    c) Spook

    d) Screech

    e) Choo-Choo

    f) Fancy-Fancy

17. What was the name of the London theatre associated with William Shakespeare?

a) The Globe

b) The Artichoke

c) The Odeon

18. In the 1950s TV series, who was the King of the Wild Frontier?

19. Which Australian soap opera is set in Summer Bay?

a) *Home and Away*

b) *The Young Doctors*

c) *Prisoner: Cell Block H*

20. Which Hollywood romantic lead was born Archie Leach?

a) Cary Grant

b) Hugh Grant

c) Russell Grant

21. Where was Elvis Presley in 1969?

a) Under the boardwalk

b) In the ghetto

c) In the gateau

22. What was the name of Robinson Crusoe's servant?

a) Man Friday

b) Mrs Thursday

c) Ruby Tuesday

23. Which of these has never been a character in the board game Cluedo?

a) Professor Plum

b) Reverend Green

c) Professor Green

24. True or false? In his university days, Walter Cronkite was once arrested for being dressed as a sheep in a public place.

25. Vince and Muskie assisted which respected American law enforcer?

a) Judge Judy

b) Theo Kojak

c) Deputy Dawg

26. Which of these was the title of a book by Charles Dickens?

a) *Little Women*

b) *Little Dorrit*

c) *Little Eva*

27. Whom did Kenny Rogers beg not to take her love to town in the title of his 1969 hit?

28. What was folk singer Roger Whittaker famous for doing to music?

a) Yodelling

b) Whistling

c) Burping

29. Who was Sherlock Holmes' arch-enemy?

a) Moriarty

b) Bluebottle

c) Hercules Grytpype-Thynne

30. Who starred opposite Ryan O'Neal in *Love Story*?

a) Ally McBeal

b) Kirstie Alley

c) Ali MacGraw

31. True or false? Cross-eyed silent-movie star Ben Turpin took out an insurance policy which would pay out $25,000 if his eyes ever became normal again.

32. Which of these was an American soul singer who died in 1984?

a) Jackie Wilson

b) Jocky Wilson

c) Ricky Wilson

33. Who played a fairy godmother in the video for Adam and the Ants' 'Prince Charming'?

a) Diana Dors

b) Barbara Windsor

c) Barbara Cartland

d) Queen Elizabeth, the Queen Mother

34. Of which future movie star did Howard Hughes once say: 'He'll never get any place, this guy. With those ears he looks like a taxi cab with both doors open'?

35. Which Canadian new-wave band had a 1980 hit with 'Echo Beach'?

a) Martha and the Muffins

b) Martha and the Cupcakes

c) Martha and the Danish Pastries

36. Which actress once said: 'Careful grooming can take twenty years off a woman's age, but you can't fool a flight of stairs'?

a) Bette Davis

b) Marlene Dietrich

c) Lana Turner

37. In her 1999 song, Shania Twain exclaimed 'Man! I Feel Like a ...'

a) Woman

b) Love machine

c) Cheese and ham bagel

38. True or false? Norwegian playwright Henrik Ibsen used to keep a pet scorpion on his desk for inspiration.

39. Which Canadian singer/ songwriter was once accused of creating music that 'gives you the feeling that your dog just died'?

a) Bryan Adams

b) Alanis Morissette

c) Leonard Cohen

Answers on page 214

FOOD AND DRINK

1. *Kopi luwak*, **one of the world's most expensive coffees, is made from which luxury ingredient?**

a) Albanian truffles

b) Mongolian snowberries

c) Indonesian civet cat poo

2. If you ordered *pesca* **ice cream in Italy, what flavour would you expect to get?**

a) Peach

b) Pear

c) Fish

3. Which of these is one of the world's hottest chillis?

a) Somerset Blaster

b) Carolina Reaper

c) Queensland Buttockclencher

4. True or false? The cookery term 'reduce the wine' means drink two-thirds of the bottle before the next step of the recipe.

5. Who once said: 'Everything you see, I owe to spaghetti'?

a) Sophia Loren

b) Marilyn Monroe

c) Orson Welles

6. George was surprised when his wife served him a sandwich containing something called 'turkey ham'. On further investigation, what did he discover that turkey ham was?

a) Ham pressed into the shape of a turkey

b) Processed turkey meat pressed into the shape of a ham

c) The meat produced by carefully mating a pig with a turkey

7. What is James Bond's favourite drink?

a) Martini cocktail

b) Pint of stout

c) Dr Pepper

8. Which one of these is not a type of pasta?

a) Vermicelli

b) Tortellini

c) Fellini

d) Radiatori

e) Fusilli

9. Which one of these statements is true?

a) The father of Spice Girl Mel C called her Melanie because melons are his favourite fruit

b) A Bulgarian woman turned purple after eating too much beetroot and then had to drink eighty gallons of milk so that her skin reverted to a paler shade of pink

c) A six-year-old Dorset boy became so addicted to Spam that he ate his way through six tins of the stuff every week for three years and had to be sent to a child psychiatrist

10. If you were a Beaune idol, you would be a fan of a wine produced in which wine growing region of France?

11. The Sardinian cheese *casu marzu* contains hundreds of what?

a) Holes

b) Blue veins

c) Live maggots

12. Which country consumes the most Coca-Cola per capita in the world?

a) Iceland

b) Japan

c) Albania

13. Who said: 'I only take a drink on two occasions – when I'm thirsty and when I'm not'?

a) Oliver Reed

b) Brendan Behan

c) Betty Ford

14. What food was thought to be poisonous until the 1830s?

a) Onion

b) Tomato

c) Spinach

15. True or false? Jussipussi is a brand of Finnish bread.

16. What is an ice lolly known as in North America?

a) Cuticle

b) Popsicle

c) Icicle

17. Which of these is not a Scottish whisky distillery?

a) Glenfiddich

b) Glenmorangie

c) Glenmatlock

18. Which of these is a popular Middle Eastern dish?

a) Humus

b) Hummus

c) Humbugs

19. The distinctive bottle of which Portuguese rosé wine was often converted into a table lamp in the 1970s?

20. Who was Dom Pérignon, after whom the champagne is named?

a) A Portuguese fisherman

b) A French Benedictine monk

c) A Spanish bullfighter

21. **What food is hurled as a highly competitive sport in Scotland and Australia?**

   a) Haggis

   b) Cheeseburger (in sesame seed bun)

   c) Blancmange

22. **True or false? Feta cheese takes its name from the Greek word for 'feet', which it smells like.**

23. **In 1990, Marathon chocolate bars changed their name to what in the UK to align with the rest of the world?**

   a) Lion

   b) Dime

   c) Snickers

24. **What animal is sometimes roasted and served whole as part of a Bedouin wedding feast?**

   a) Camel

   b) Vulture

   c) Centipede

25. **John Harvey Kellogg introduced corn flakes as a breakfast cereal in the nineteenth century in the hope that they would do what?**

   a) Stimulate hair growth

   b) Boost mental capacity

   c) Reduce masturbation

Answers on page 214

SPORT

1. Which one of these is a popular Turkish sport?

   a) Camel football

   b) Camel wrestling

   c) Camel skating

2. On which island do the international TT motorcycle races take place?

   a) Isle of Man

   b) Sri Lanka

   c) Corfu

3. What colour did South African Gary Player always wear on the golf course?

   a) Black

   b) Red

   c) Beige

4. True or false? Baseball legend Babe Ruth used to wear a cabbage leaf on his head to keep him cool on the field.

5. What is the nickname of the Australian rugby union team?

   a) Kangaroos

   b) Wallabies

   c) Wombats

6. What do you call a score of two under par on a golf hole?

a) A birdie

b) An eagle

c) A miracle

7. Before finding fame as a singer, Johnny Mathis excelled at which track and field event?

a) Pole vault

b) Hammer throw

c) High jump

8. Why is American golfer Craig Stadler affectionately known as 'the walrus'?

a) He eats a lot of fish

b) He has an ample build and a bushy moustache

c) He has two prominent front teeth

9. Which one of these statements is true?

a) The captain of an Argentine football team was injured during the toss of the coin when the referee, making room for the drop, accidentally trod on the player's foot and put him out of action for three weeks

b) A Brazilian goalkeeper once let in a goal after three seconds to a shot from the half-way line while he was still on his knees in the goalmouth saying his pre-match prayer

c) A Uruguayan defender was so incensed by a referee's decision that he chased the hapless official out of the stadium and two miles down the road before losing him in a maze of streets

10. In swimming, what is the front crawl also known as?

a) Doggie paddle

b) Doggie bowl

c) Doggie style

11. Deportivo Morón is a soccer team from which country?

a) Argentina

b) Spain

c) Peru

12. American boxer Harry Greb overcame what handicap to become world middleweight champion for three years from 1923 to 1926?

a) He only had one leg

b) He was blind in one eye

c) He had a metal hook in place of his left hand

13. What is golfer Tiger Woods' real first name?

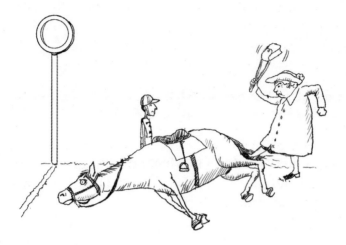

14. Which horse owned by Queen Elizabeth the Queen Mother collapsed in a heap yards from the finish line while leading the 1956 Grand National?

a) Arkle

b) Devon Loch

c) Mister Ed

15. Valentino Rossi is a multiple world champion in which sport?

a) Motorcycling

b) Trampolining

c) Pool

16. Which of these is the name of an Australian Test cricket ground?

a) The Bugga

b) The Yucca

c) The Gabba

17. Which sport would you play at Devils Knob, Three Little Bakers, Possum Trot, Kissing Camels and Useless Bay?

a) Golf

b) Baseball

c) Polo

18. True or false? Former British boxing champion Henry Cooper had an identical twin brother named Gary.

19. A 'frozen rope' is a term in which sport?

a) Baseball

b) Ice fishing

c) Bungee jumping

20. What were the very first ice hockey pucks made from?

a) Large stones

b) Frozen burgers

c) Frozen cow dung

21. What is a period of play in polo called – a pukka or a chukka?

22. What was American tennis player Billie Jean King's maiden name?

a) Jackson

b) Moffitt

c) Spears

23. Of which colourful US basketball player famous for his nose piercings did Bob Costas once say: 'He has so many fish hooks in his nose, he looks like a piece of bait'?

24.The Coventry Bees, the Poole Pirates and the King's Lynn Stars are all teams in which sport?

a) Basketball

b) Ice hockey

c) Speedway

25. True or false? Former French Formula One driver Jean Behra used to keep a spare plastic right ear in his pocket during races.

26. Geoff Capes represented Great Britain at the 1972, 1976 and 1980 Olympics in which event?

a) Shot put

b) Discus

c) Triple jump

27. In which sport did a mass underwater brawl break out between the USSR and Hungary at the 1956 Olympics?

a) Water polo

b) Diving

c) Synchronized swimming

28. What was the nickname of American footballer William Perry?

a) The Boiler

b) The Refrigerator

c) The Fitted Wardrobe

29. What was the name of the goalkeeper in Great Britain's victorious 2016 Olympic women's hockey team?

a) Alex Danson

b) Maddie Hinch

c) Josephine Hart

30. What is the fastest recorded pit stop in Formula One?

a) 1.92 seconds

b) 3.2 seconds

c) 'Let me see now, can you collect it on Thursday?'

31. Which temperamental US tennis player, who won three Wimbledon men's singles titles in the 1980s, was once described as having 'hair like badly turned broccoli'?

32. In which cities do the following football teams play?

a) Lazio

b) Boca Juniors

c) Arsenal

d) Real Sociedad

e) Juventus

f) Dynamo Moscow

Answers on page 214

GEOGRAPHY

1. Which of these is the name of a city in the American state of New Mexico?

a) Postman's Knock

b) Blind Man's Buff

c) Truth or Consequences

2. What does the name of the village of Muckanaghederdauhaulia in County Tipperary, Ireland, mean?

a) Land of the little people

b) Piggery between two briny places

c) You can see New York on a clear day

3. True or false? The Cheddar Gorge is made entirely of cheese.

4. What commodity is celebrated annually by way of a festival in Talkeetna, Alaska?

   a) Moose droppings

   b) Paper clips

   c) Hair extensions

5. Which colourful pattern takes its popular name from a Scottish town situated a few miles to the west of Glasgow?

6. Near which city would you find Bondi Beach?

   a) Mumbai

   b) Rio de Janeiro

   c) Sydney

7. True or false? Nowhere is a small community in Oklahoma.

8. If George drives due north from Wyoming, what is the first state he would come to ... provided his wife isn't map-reading and he isn't too proud to stop and ask for directions?

   a) Colorado

   b) Montana

   c) Nebraska

9. What is the capital of New Zealand?

   a) Wellington

   b) Auckland

   c) Shanghai

10. Where might you expect to find Arthur's Seat?

   a) Belfast

   b) Edinburgh

   c) At the top of Arthur's legs

11. The name of which American state is abbreviated to MO?

12. Complete the Irish proverb: 'Bare walls make ...'

   a) Sleep hard to come by

   b) A job for a husband

   c) Giddy housekeepers

13. What do you call a native of the French region of Alsace?

   a) Aleutian

   b) Alsatian

   c) Doberman Pinscher

14. True or false? It is illegal to make 'ugly faces' at dogs in the state of Oklahoma.

15. Which of these is not the name of a river in Australia?

   a) Sweetheart

   b) Darling

   c) Love

16. Which Irish city gives its name to a five-line rhyme?

17. In 1992, the Norwegian town of Bodo staged the world's first festival of what?

   a) Verrucas

   b) Divorce

   c) Grandmothers

18. Verulamium was the Roman name for which English city?

a) St Albans

b) Bath

c) Milton Keynes

19. What are the only two countries in the world whose names start with an 'A' but don't end with one?

20. According to local superstition, what is considered bad luck to allow on a fishing boat on the Mediterranean island of Ibiza?

a) A pregnant woman

b) A priest

c) A great white shark

21. The name of which capital city translates from Latin as 'I see a mountain'?

a) Reykjavik

b) Montevideo

c) Amsterdam

22. Which of these is the name of a village in Cornwall?

a) Mousetrap

b) Mousetail

c) Mousehole

23. True or false? Norway once held a full public referendum to decide what colour dress their queen should wear on a forthcoming state visit to Denmark.

24. Of what was Hawaii once the world's leading producer?

a) Surf boards

b) Pineapples

c) Steve McGarrett impersonators

25. In which US state is Kansas City?

a) Kansas

b) Missouri

c) Wyoming

26. What landmark has its address at 1600 Pennsylvania Avenue, Washington, DC?

a) The Lincoln Memorial

b) The White House

c) Disneyland

27. As part of an international day of celebration, what are you encouraged to do to your houseplant on 27 July each year?

a) Give it a bath in luxury oils

b) Take it for a walk

c) Sing to it

Answers on page 215

WORDS

1. What would you do with a balalaika?

a) Play it

b) Put it on your head

c) Milk it

2. What word links water, leg and twelve times?

3. If you are ostracized by people, you are said to be sent to which English city?

a) Chelmsford

b) Coventry

c) Stoke-on-Trent

4. George's wife told him he was 'gongoozling'. Does this mean he was?

a) Staring idly into space

b) Playing with himself

c) Spending too much time on the Internet

5. What word can mean an association of people united by a common interest, or a heavy wooden stick?

6. What would you hit with a niblick?

a) Your knee

b) A nail

c) A golf ball

7. True or false? 'Negligent' is a condition in which you absent-mindedly answer the door while wearing your nightdress.

8. What do couples traditionally present to each other to celebrate their twentieth wedding anniversary?

a) Pearl

b) China

c) Cheese and onion crisps

9. What word goes before ball, rate and line?

10. George told his wife that he was having problems with his dongle. Did she advise him to go to?

a) The doctor

b) A gentlemen's outfitters

c) A computer repair shop

11. If you are bitten by a poisonous snake, is it better for the doctor to give you an antidote or an anecdote?

12. In order to safeguard the legal status of animals, several politically correct organizations have suggested that 'pet owners' should now be referred to as what?

a) Pet projects

b) Pet guardians

c) Pet cohabitors

13. What word can go before chair, toothbrush and blanket?

14. Which of these is North American slang for a detective?

a) Slipper

b) Plimsoll

c) Gumshoe

15. If you had salopettes, would you?

a) Wear them

b) Cook them

c) Put some cream on them

16. George said it was pleasantly warm outside. Did he mean the weather was balmy or barmy?

17. Sylvia's husband told her she was a right smellfungus. Why might this be considered grounds for divorce?

a) It means she is hyper-critical about almost everything

b) It calls into question her personal hygiene

c) It suggests she is an incorrigible gossip

18. What is the collective noun for a group of owls?

  a) Congress

  b) Parliament

  c) Senate

19. True or false? At school, Paul McCartney was the only boy in his class who could spell the word 'phlegm'.

20. What is brontology the study of?

  a) The Bronte sisters

  b) The brontosaurus

  c) Thunder

21. If you decide to give up drink, might you be trying to?

  a) Exercise your demons

  or

  b) Exorcize your demons

22. Why did Sylvia look puzzled when her brother told her that accusations that he was having an affair were just a 'pigment of her imagination'?

23. If you were caught short in the Australian bush, would you use?

  a) A dunny

  b) A tucker bag

  c) A didgeridoo

24. What name links Sellers, Falk and Perfect?

25. Sylvia's brother said he was in great pain because he had 'a nasty abbess on his knee'. Given that he had been nowhere near a convent, what word did he mean to use?

26. What would you do with a kumquat?

  a) Eat it

  b) Polish it

  c) Ride it

27. George's father used to regale everyone with tales of the poverty and hardship he had to endure when he was young. 'I had a depraved childhood,' he would announce solemnly. Why did the rest of the family snigger and what word did he mean to use?

Answers on page 215

SECTION 3

You pride yourself on being down with the kids and are just thankful that it's a spiritual rather than a physical state because bending down is no longer your strong point. You reckon there's no way that you're over the hill yet, even though your birth certificate suggests you have a pretty good view of the summit. You know your Tinchy Stryder from your Tinie Tempah and snigger at contemporaries who think Kanye West is a train station. So let's test your cool credentials.

HISTORY

1. Where was the skeleton of English king Richard III discovered in 2012?

a) Beneath a car park

b) At a bus stop

c) Slumped on his throne at the battlefield of Bosworth having been told by the royal horse-seller: 'Please hold. Your call is important to us.'

2. Who was the vice president of the United States from 1969 to 1973 under Richard Nixon?

a) Hunter S. Thompson

b) Spiro T. Agnew

c) Wile E. Coyote

3. What was discovered on the moon in 2009?

a) Water

b) Shergar

c) A shopping cart

4. What name is shared by the prime minister of Rhodesia from 1964 to 1979 and the actor who played Harold Bishop in *Neighbours*?

5. What is the name of Bill Clinton's wife?

a) Chelsea

b) Hillary

c) Monica

6.Who was beaten by Hillary Clinton for the 2016 Democratic US presidential nomination?

a) Bernie Madoff

b) Bernie Ecclestone

c) Bernie Sanders

7. True or false? Diminutive former French president Nicolas Sarkozy used to order his statuesque wife, Carla Bruni, to kneel in all official photographs so that they could appear in frame together.

8. Who became leader of North Korea in 2011?

a) Kim Jong-un

b) Kim Jong-deux

c) Kim Jong-trois

9. Of which US president did Robin Williams comment: 'People say satire is dead. It's not dead; it's alive and living in the White House'?

10. Which actor served as the thirty-eighth governor of California from 2003 to 2011?

a) Tom Cruise

b) Arnold Schwarzenegger

c) Will Ferrell

11. Which of the following has been prime minister of Australia?

a) Tony Abbott

b) Russ Abbot

c) Abbott and Costello

12. In 1985, Wham! became the first Western pop band to do what?

a) Eat sushi

b) Perform a gig in communist China

c) Dance bare-chested in a tank as part of the Soviet Union May Day Parade

13. True or false? Former mayor of London Ken Livingstone has had a lifelong fascination with newts.

14. What is the name of Queen Elizabeth II's youngest son?

a) Andrew

b) Edward

c) Wayne

15. Who was elected chancellor of Germany in 2005?

a) Willy Brandt

b) Angela Merkel

c) Franz Beckenbauer

16. Which US president, taking office in 1977, was dismissed by his opponents as a peanut farmer?

17. What brought Britain and France closer in 1994?

a) The Channel Tunnel opened

b) The derogatory term *les rosbifs* was outlawed by the French government

c) The beret became a major UK fashion item

18. Ronald Reagan's first wife, Jane Wyman, starred in which American TV series?

a) *The Beverly Hillbillies*

b) *Falcon Crest*

c) *Happy Days*

19. In 2006, what was spotted swimming in the River Thames for the first time since 1913?

a) A polar bear

b) A whale

c) Dame Vera Lynn

20. True or false? US politician Al Gore is the son of Lesley Gore, and following the Democrats' controversial defeat in the 2000 presidential election, they duetted together on her Sixties hit 'It's My Party and I'll Cry If I Want To'.

21. What was completed around London in 1986 with a view to keeping traffic out of the capital?

a) An electric fence

b) A moat

c) The M25

22. What system was introduced by the banking industry supposedly to improve personal security when using debit or credit cards in machines?

a) Chip and Pin

b) Hit and Hope

c) Press and Pray

23. Which battle where England famously defeated France celebrated its 600th anniversary in 2015?

24. Which of these has not been leader of the Scottish National Party?

a) Nicola Sturgeon

b) Alex Salmond

c) Richard Herring

25. What device was Austria's Felix Baumgartner wearing in 2012 when he descended to Earth from an altitude of 128,000 feet at a speed of over 800mph?

a) A parachute

b) Underpants loaded with two sticks of dynamite

c) A 16-ton weight

26. Which Fergie is a parent of Princesses Beatrice and Eugenie?

a) Sarah Ferguson

b) Fergie from the Black Eyed Peas

c) Sir Alex Ferguson

27. Of whom did Irving Layton say: 'Canada has at last produced a political leader worthy of assassination'?

28. Whose face can be found on an Australian $100 note?

a) Dame Nellie Melba

b) Dame Edna Everage

c) Skippy the bush kangaroo

29. Who was head of Britain's Joint Intelligence Committee at the time of the 'dodgy dossier' that made a case for the Iraq War?

a) John Scarlett

b) Miss Scarlett

c) Captain Scarlet

30. Ban Ki-moon was elected secretary-general of which organization in 2006?

a) International Banking Federation

b) United Nations

c) FIFA

Answers on page 215

SCIENCE AND NATURE

1. Which of these is a social media site on the Internet?

    a) Bebo

    b) Devo

    c) Nemo

2. True or false? Nagware is the name given to computer software that is free for a trial period and then frequently reminds the user to pay for it.

3. The name of which animal is used to describe an older woman who enjoys romantic liaisons with much younger men?

    a) Hyena

    b) Cougar

    c) Cheetah

4. Which one of the following has yet to be blamed on climate change?

    a) Warmer weather

    b) Wetter weather

    c) Drier weather

    d) Windier weather

    e) Calmer weather

    f) Donald Trump's election as US president

5. If a gentleman was described as possessing 'moobs', would he be considered overweight or underweight in the chest department?

6. Inventor James Dyson is best known for producing which household device?

   a) Vacuum cleaner

   b) Lawn mower

   c) Electric nose hair remover

7. True or false? In 2016, Russia banned all robins from the country on the grounds that their song was interpreted as blatant political criticism of the old Stalinist regime.

8. What was the name of the sheep that became the world's first cloned mammal in 1996?

   a) Molly

   b) Polly

   c) Dolly

9. How did Tian Tian, a female giant panda at Edinburgh Zoo, disappoint zoo officials in 2014?

   a) She did not become pregnant

   b) She totally went off bamboo and started ordering sweet and sour pork instead

   c) She announced that she was fed up with wearing monochrome because it was so last season

10. True or false? Kangaroos are excellent swimmers and have been found swimming a mile out to sea off the coast of Australia.

11. Which of these is the name of a digital optical disc data storage format (yes I know, me neither), which was designed to be an improvement on the DVD?

a) Blu-tack

b) Blu-ray

c) Sting-ray

12. Which planet was cruelly demoted to 'dwarf planet' status in 2006?

13. Which one of these creatures was not on the WWF endangered species list for 2016?

a) Black rhino

b) Mountain gorilla

c) Ant

14. Which of these products is not made by Apple?

a) iPad

b) iPod

c) iLiner

d) iPhone

15. True or false? Ferret-legging is a popular Yorkshire endurance test where competitors remove their underwear and stand for as long as they can bear it with a live ferret tucked down each leg of their trousers.

16. Which of these men co-founded Microsoft?

a) Bill Gates

b) Steve Jobs

c) Joey Essex

17. What have climate experts predicted that our grandchildren may never see again after the year 2050?

a) Wasps

b) Snow

c) 2049

18. What is 'app' short for?

a) Appendix

b) Apparatus

c) Application

19. In 2016, a newly discovered species of tarantula was named after which iconic country singer?

a) Dolly Parton

b) Willie Nelson

c) Johnny Cash

20. If you are targeted by Internet bullies, what are you said to be the victim of?

a) Imps

b) Gremlins

c) Trolls

21. True or false? Piers Morgan's ego is visible on Google Earth.

22. Which of these is not a genuine shrub?

a) Bourbon Rose

b) Iggy Azalea

c) *Camellia japonica*

23. Which of these is an Internet search engine?

a) Yoohoo

b) Yahoo

c) Atchoo

Answers on page 215

MATHS

1. **What number do you get if you divide Jay-Z's problems by Eddie Cochran's steps to heaven?**

2. George's broadband provider promised him a speed of 16.0Mb, but the best he ever gets is 3.3Mb. By how many Mb is George missing out on the advertised speed, and is this why steam can be seen coming out of his ears whenever he tries to access the Internet?

3. **How many months in 2015 contained twenty-eight days?**

4. A woman in Sylvia's street was married five times, but three of her spouses ended up dead. Expressed as a percentage, how many of her husbands lived to wed another day?

5. **George does four Sudoku puzzles every Sunday and three Sudoku puzzles on every other day of the week. How many Sudoku puzzles does he do in a week, and how long will it be before he loses the will to live?**

6. How many 50 Cents are there in Dollar?

7. George's broadband provider boasts that 75 per cent of its customers are satisfied with its service. It has six million customers. How many dissatisfied, angry or routinely hacked off customers does it have (including George)?

8. What is 10 per cent of *Fifty Shades of Grey*?

9. George's friend Alec doesn't like to be rushed into adopting new technology, which is why he listens to music on a cassette player, has a mobile phone the size of a brick and was still running Windows 97 in 2016. How many years out of date was his computer software program?

10. George's first computer password was DopeyBashfulAladdinCinderellaTomJerryBatman because he read that it had to contain seven characters. Without taking your shoes and socks off, calculate by how many letters George exceeded the limit.

11. Eighties pop: what number would you be left with if you subtracted Level 42 from Haircut 100?

12. On a two-week holiday in Cyprus with her friends, George's granddaughter drank two bottles of wine and five shots every night. Over the course of the fortnight, how many bottles of wine and shots did she consume, and as a percentage how much of her holiday does she remember?

Answers on page 216

THE ARTS

1. Which of these is not a celebrity couple (as of January 2017)?

a) David and Victoria Beckham

b) Michael and Sarah Palin

c) Ozzy and Sharon Osbourne

2. Which of these is the name of a US pop rock band?

a) Manson

b) Hanson

c) Henson

3. Which of these was not a member of the Sex Pistols?

a) Sid Vicious

b) Bobby Crush

c) Johnny Rotten

4. True or false? Blur singer Damon Albarn was actually born Damon Albran but changed his name to avoid confusion with the high-fibre breakfast cereal.

5. Leslie Knope is the central character in which US TV comedy?

a) *Parks and Recreation*

b) *Will and Grace*

c) *The Big Bang Theory*

6. Which female pop singer would you get if you mixed Simply Red with the White Stripes?

7. Which of these is not the title of a Tom Hanks film?

a) *Saving Mr. Banks*

b) *Saving Private Ryan*

c) *Saving Ryan's Privates*

8. Whereas in our day fans of the Beatles were just called 'Beatles fans', today's star turns give special names to their followers, such as the 'Directioners' who worship what's left of boy band One Direction. So what name is given to people who are irrationally taken with the following?

a) Justin Bieber

b) Taylor Swift

c) Katy Perry

9. Who retired from hosting NBC's *Tonight Show* in 2014 after a twenty-two-year stint?

a) David Letterman

b) Jay Leno

c) Larry King

10. Walter White was the notorious chemist turned drug baron in which TV series?

a) *The Wire*

b) *Breaking Bad*

c) *The Waltons*

11. Which 2008 film tells the fictional story of eighteen-year-old Jamal Malik, a contestant on the Indian version of *Who Wants To Be a Millionaire?*

12. Which of these is the name of a Canadian rock band?

a) Dollarback

b) Nickelback

c) Stickleback

13. Actress Whoopi Goldberg once worked as what?

a) Lavatory attendant

b) Tax collector

c) Beautician in a morgue

14. True or false? *Homes Under the Hamas* **is a popular daytime property show on Palestinian TV.**

15. The second *Pirates of the Caribbean* **movie was titled** *Dead Man's ...*

a) *Chest*

b) *Dentures*

c) *Ashes*

16. Which of these is a long-running character in the Australian soap *Neighbours***?**

a) Toadie

b) Froggy

c) Newt

17. Hugh Jackman stars as which comic book character in the *X-Men* **series of films?**

a) Tapir

b) Capybara

c) Wolverine

18. **Which of these waterproof items was the subject of a 2007 worldwide hit for Rihanna?**

a) Umbrella

b) Sou'wester

c) Gum boots

19. **A. J. McLean, Howie D, Nick Carter, Kevin Richardson and Brian Littrell make up which US boy band?**

a) The Backstreet Boys

b) New Kids on the Block

c) Megadeth

20. **Michael Hutchence was the lead singer with which Australian rock band?**

21. **Which rapper had a UK number one in 2008 with 'American Boy'?**

a) Estelle

b) Estelle Getty

c) Don Estelle

22. **Which of these is a major character in *The Hunger Games* trilogy by Suzanne Collins?**

a) Katniss

b) Katnip

c) Katnap

d) Kitkat

23. **Which of these is an American pop singer?**

a) Jessica Simpson

b) Jessica Lange

c) Jessica Rabbit

24. Which of these was a member of the cast of *Friends*?

a) Lisa Simpson

b) Lisa Kudrow

c) Lisa Vanderpump

25. What was different about the winner of the 2014 Eurovision Song Contest?

a) He sang the winning entry while baking a Victoria sponge

b) He was a bearded woman

c) He sang in tune

26. What does Forrest Gump's mother compare life to in the film of the same name?

a) A box of matches

b) A box of chocolates

c) A box of frogs

27. True or false? Overly temperamental Russian ballerinas have their own special dance troupe, the Bolshie Ballet.

28. Which of these is a popular video game apparently capable of entertaining young people for hours?

a) *Angry Birds*

b) *Angry Bees*

c) *Angry Badgers*

29. Jon Snow is a major character in which TV series?

a) *The West Wing*

b) *Game of Thrones*

c) *Family Guy*

30. True or false? Former First Lady Barbara Bush has a signed tattoo of Slash from Guns N' Roses on her left buttock.

31. Who provides the voice of Donkey in the movie *Shrek*?

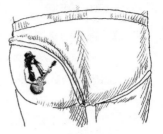

a) Alec Baldwin

b) Eddie Murphy

c) Dan Quayle

32. Caleb, Nathan, Jared and Matthew Followill make up which rock band?

a) Maroon 5

b) AC/DC

c) Kings of Leon

33. Whose 2016 autobiography was titled *Born to Run*?

a) Bruce Springsteen

b) Michael Johnson

c) Carl Lewis

34. Buzz Lightyear is a heroic character in which series of films?

a) *Star Wars*

b) *The Lord of the Rings*

c) *Toy Story*

35. Which of these is not the name of a girl band?

a) Sugababes

b) Destiny's Child

c) The Ramones

36. True or false? Puerto Rican singer Ricky Martin took a break from 'Livin' la Vida Loca' to come to Britain and win the 2012 series of *The Apprentice*.

37. Which US TV game show has Vanna White co-presented since 1982?

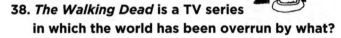

a) *The Price is Right*

b) *Wheel of Fortune*

c) *Wheel of Torture*

38. *The Walking Dead* is a TV series in which the world has been overrun by what?

a) Centipedes

b) Zombies

c) Senior citizens

39. Which of these musicians did not die in 2016?

a) David Bowie

b) Prince

c) Leonard Cohen

d) Glenn Frey

e) Ludwig van Beethoven

40. How many Kardashian sisters can you name? Clue: there are five (including two half-sisters) and their names all begin with the same letter: K.

41. Sylvia's sister can often be heard moaning about that 'Justin Beaver'. Can you correct these other malapropisms that suggest her knowledge of contemporary music may contain one or two gaps?

a) Little Minx

b) Dildo

c) Justin Timberwolf

d) Food Fighters

e) Mary J. Bilge

f) Our Kelly

Answers on page 216

FOOD AND DRINK

1. Which of these is a German pizza-manufacturing company?

   a) Dr Feelgood

   b) Dr Crippen

   c) Dr Oetker

2. True or false? Arachibutyrophobia is a fear of peanut butter sticking to the roof of your mouth.

3. Which of these is the name of a thick Scottish soup made from haddock, potatoes and onions?

   a) Cullen stink

   b) Cullen skink

   c) Cullen skunk

4. If you ordered 'moules' in a French restaurant, what would you be eating?

5. What was voted Britain's favourite regional dish in 2016?

   a) Cornish pasty

   b) Yorkshire pudding

   c) Suffolk punch

6. **True or false? At a bathroom-themed restaurant in Taiwan, customers sit on toilet seats instead of chairs.**

7. **What did the ancient Egyptians believe would be kept away by mixing half an onion with beer foam?**

    a) Salespeople

    b) Death

    c) Everyone

8. **How many hard-boiled eggs can American competitive eater Joey 'Jaws' Chestnut consume in eight minutes and is this why it is advisable not to stand downwind of him for the next twenty-four hours?**

    a) 73

    b) 109

    c) 141

9. **Which of these is a variety of melon?**

    a) Cantaloupe

    b) Cantilever

    c) Antelope

10. **What is the most popular pizza topping in the US?**

11. **What did Blanche of Navarre send to twelfth-century French king Philippe Auguste every year in the hope of winning his heart?**

    a) A consignment of oysters

    b) 200 blocks of cheese

    c) A giant box of chocolates (with the coffee creams taken out)

12. **True or false? The world's biggest burger, served at a bar in Michigan, weighs 185 pounds – 740 times the size of the average quarter pounder.**

13. Which one of these is not the name of a brand of beer?

a) Old Speckled Hen

b) Fiddler's Elbow

c) Theakston's Old Peculier

d) Sick Duck

e) Mangled Marmoset

f) Arrogant Bastard

14. Which of these is an edible grain crop originally from South America?

a) Ectozoa

b) Quinoa

c) Jerboa

15. What is Bastardo del Grappa?

a) An Italian cheese

b) A Spanish liqueur

c) A moody sommelier

16. Innocent Bystander, Soldier's Block and The Listening Station are all winemakers from which country?

17. Sylvia returned from her holiday in Mexico with a red snapper. Had she been?

a) Shopping in a fish market

b) Shopping in a fruit market

c) Sunbathing naked for too long without factor 30

18. What are the two principal ingredients of banoffee pie?

a) Steak and kidney

b) Cheese and tomato

c) Banana and toffee

19. Which of these is the name for a French pot usually used for cooking casseroles?

a) Marmot

b) Marmite

c) Marsupial

20. Chassagne-Montrachet and Meursault are elegant varieties of what?

a) White port

b) White wine

c) White cider

21. True or false? Singing diva Mariah Carey is addicted to Rich Tea biscuits – and for her 2008 world tour she demanded that the walls of every hotel room in which she stayed should be covered with thousands of Rich Tea wrappers.

22. In 2016, what was voted Britain's favourite sandwich?

a) Bacon

b) Prawn

c) Crispy stoat with mayo

23. How many bars of chocolate does the average Swiss person consume in a year?

a) 120

b) 240

c) 360

24. Which of these is not a vegetarian option?

a) Stuffed peppers

b) Stuffed tofu

c) Stuffed venison

25. Which of these champagne bottle sizes is the largest in volume?

a) Methuselah

b) Jeroboam

c) Nebuchadnezzar

26. True or false? Jellied moose nose is considered a delicacy in parts of northern Canada.

27. Which celebrity lent his name to a successful model of fat-reducing grill?

a) George Foreman

b) George Formby

c) George Michael

28. In which country is a beer named Vergina brewed?

a) Uruguay

b) Korea

c) Greece

Answers on page 216

SPORT

1. Which Spanish soccer club plays at the Bernabeu Stadium?

a) Barcelona

b) Real Madrid

c) Sevilla

2. Which of these is the name of an American professional golfer who competed at the 2016 Masters?

a) Happy Hermann

b) Smylie Kaufman

c) Jollee Anderson

3. Why is snooker player John Higgins known as 'The Wizard of Wishaw'?

a) He is a fully licensed wizard

b) He is a big Harry Potter fan

c) He comes from Wishaw in Scotland

4. How many Olympic gold medals has American swimmer Michael Phelps won?

a) 13

b) 18

c) 23

5. What is the name of Michael Schumacher's brother, who also drove in Formula One?

a) Ralf

b) Alf

c) Helmut

6. Which of these is not the name of a ball game?

a) Korfball

b) Dodgeball

c) Amazeballs

7. True or false?
A pantomime horse finished a plucky ninth in the 2011 Grand National.

8. What was the nickname of US tennis player Pete Sampras?

a) Pistol Pete

b) Shotgun Pete

c) Texas Pete

9. Who said: 'If there's a thunderstorm on a golf course, walk down the middle of the fairway, holding a one-iron over your head. Even God can't hit a one-iron'?

a) John Daly

b) Nick Faldo

c) Lee Trevino

10. Which of these is the name of a US baseball team?

a) Philadelphia Freedom

b) Philadelphia Cheesies

c) Philadelphia Phillies

11. LeBron James is one of the world's richest sportsmen. Which sport does he play professionally?

a) Basketball

b) American football

c) Conkers

12. Who won a sailing gold medal for Australia at the 2016 Olympics?

a) Tim Burton

b) Tom Burton

c) Richard Burton

13. How many points do you get for a try in rugby union?

14. Who did Andy Murray defeat in the 2013 Wimbledon men's singles final to become the first Briton to win the men's title for seventy-seven years?

a) Roger Federer

b) Novak Djokovic

c) Christopher Biggins

15. What was the nickname of American golfer Jack Nicklaus?

a) The Golden Dragon

b) The Golden Fleece

c) The Golden Bear

16. Australian Olympic swimming champion Ian Thorpe owes much of his success to his extra-large feet. What shoe size are they?

a) 15

b) 17

c) 25

17. Which country staged the 2016 European Football Championship, or Euro 2016?

a) Spain

b) France

c) Argentina

18. True or false? Both Felipe Massa and Felipe Nasr were Brazilian drivers in the 2016 Formula One season.

19. The 800-metre runner Gaylord Silly represented which country at the 2012 World Indoor Athletics Championships?

a) United States

b) Australia

c) Seychelles

20. Which city hosts the Canadian Formula One Grand Prix?

a) Ottawa

b) Vancouver

c) Montreal

21. In which sport might you perform a lutz, an axel and a salchow?

a) Yachting

b) Figure skating

c) Darts

22. True or false? A Russian swimmer was disqualified from the 2016 world championships when it was discovered that he had a miniature outboard motor fitted in his trunks.

23. What is the name of Serena Williams's tennis-playing sister?

a) Neptune Williams

b) Venus Williams

c) Jupiter Williams

24. In 2015, who became the first female jockey to win Australia's prestigious Melbourne Cup race?

a) Michelle Payne

b) Hayley Turner

c) Madge Allsop

25. Which country hosted the 2014 Winter Olympics?

a) Russia

b) Canada

c) United Arab Emirates

26. Who scored Germany's winning goal in the 2014 World Cup final?

a) Mario Andretti

b) Mario Götze

c) Super Mario

27. Hazeltine National staged which major sports event in 2016?

a) World Cycling Championships

b) Ryder Cup

c) Preakness Stakes

28. In which sport did Joe Clarke win gold for Great Britain at the 2016 Olympics?

a) Sailing

b) Canoeing

c) Hide and Seek

Answers on page 217

GEOGRAPHY

1. Which natural granite formation in Western Australia has been shaped by wind and water?

a) Ayers Rock

b) Wave Rock

c) Punk Rock

2. What country was renamed Myanmar in 1989 by its military government?

a) Bangladesh

b) Burma

c) Wales

3. Which of these is the name of a village in Kent?

a) Fool's Butt

or

b) Pratt's Bottom

4. True or false? According to Russian superstition, if a single woman sits at the corner of a table, she won't marry for seven years.

5. What do competitors chase down Cooper's Hill in Gloucestershire, England, every year in one of the world's wackiest races?

a) A fair maiden

b) A whippet

c) A large cheese

6. Which canal connects the Atlantic Ocean to the Pacific?

a) The Suez Canal

b) The Panama Canal

c) The Alimentary Canal

7. Several American states contain a town named Manchester. Can you name any of them? Go on, guess.

8. Where would you find the city of Chihuahua?

a) Honduras

b) Mexico

c) Isle of Dogs

9. Which Atlantic island gives its name to a type of semi-casual shorts and an infamous triangle?

10. Mount Logan is the highest point in which country?

a) Canada

b) Australia

c) New Zealand

11. What is the capital of the Falkland Islands?

a) Sidney

b) Stanley

c) Ollie

12. Is Hell a town in Michigan or a weekend in Cleethorpes?

13. Estonia, Latvia and Lithuania make up which group of countries?

a) The Baltic States

b) The Balkan States

c) The Middle East

14. Leeds Castle in Kent houses a museum that contains what is thought to be the world's largest collection of what?

a) Back scratchers

b) Dog collars

c) Airline sick bags

15. Eivissa is the Catalan name for which island?

a) Formentera

b) Ibiza

c) Thanet

16. Which of these is the name of a headland located on the western edge of Swansea Bay in South Wales?

a) The Tumbles

b) The Fumbles

c) The Mumbles

17. Bratislava is the capital of which European country?

a) Slovenia

b) Slovakia

c) Moldova

18. Which of these cities is the furthest north?

a) Quebec

b) London

c) Tokyo

19. What do competitors throw at each other on the last Wednesday of August in the Spanish town of Buñol?

a) Eggs

b) Horse manure

c) Tomatoes

20. True or false? Around one-third of all road accidents on state roads in Sweden involve a moose.

21. Which one of these is not the name of a place in Australia?

a) Dumbleyung

b) Yackandandah

c) Marangaroo

d) Kyssagoolie

e) Koolyanobbing

f) Widgiemooltha

g) Humpty Doo

22. What are the three countries in Africa that have only four letters in their name?

23. Which of these gained its independence in 2011 to become the 193rd member of the United Nations?

a) South Shields

b) South Sudan

c) South Fork

Answers on page 217

WORDS

1. **Which of these has not been named Oxford Dictionaries' Word of the Year?**

    a) Selfie

    b) Reem

    c) Omnishambles

2. **Who would be the most likely to use the phrase 'pushing the envelope' – a middle manager, a postman or the world's worst strongman?**

3. **What do the initials WDYT stand for in that messaging lark that young people seem to love so much?**

    a) Who Do You Trust?

    b) What Do You Think?

    c) Why Do You Tweet?

    d) Who Dissed Your Turkey? (Christmas and Thanksgiving only)

4. **Is a metrosexual a stylish, cultured man or someone with a fetish for making love on the Circle Line?**

5. If someone tells you they are going phishing, where might you find them?

a) On a riverbank

b) Behind the bike sheds

c) At a computer

6. George's granddaughter loves her scrunchies. Does she?

a) Put milk on them and eat them out of a bowl for breakfast

or

b) Tie her hair in them

7. If your grandson told you that his new best friend was 'wicked', how many criminal convictions would you expect the friend to have?

8. If someone said you were having a 'brain fart', what would you be experiencing?

a) A senior moment

b) Embarrassing flatulence

c) The onset of verbal diarrhoea

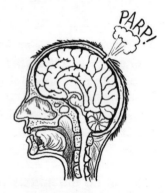

9. Sylvia was sitting opposite a young gentleman on a train when he told her he admired her fur baby. Should she ... ?

a) Thank him for complimenting her pet

or

b) Threaten to sue him for sexual harassment

10. What amalgamation of the words 'brother' and 'romance' is used to describe an intense, emotional, but non-sexual bond between two men?

11. George heard his granddaughter tell her friend she was 'well jel'. Did it mean she was ... ?

a) Wearing a lot of hair products

b) Extremely jealous

c) Full of birthday party jelly

12. What is 'totes' short for, as in 'I totes need a new dress for the ball, okay, and I saw one yesterday that was totes divine, so I totes must buy it'?

13. In modern parlance, what does NBD stand for?

a) New Black Dress

b) Nice Bazookas, Daphne

c) No Big Deal

14. Is 'lamestream' a term to define a form of media that is considered old-fashioned or a river that has dried to a trickle?

15. George's granddaughter told him that her latest boyfriend was definitely a 'keeper'. So how come, when under strict interrogation from George, the lad knew nothing about the feeding times of the sea lions at the zoo?

16. True or false? A stalemate is a husband who has lost his ardour.

17. In 2003, a High Court judge ruling on a copyright case was understandably mystified by a rap song that contained the lyric 'fo' shizzle my nizzle'. After lengthy investigations, what did he discover that it meant?

a) Blow me down with a feather

b) For sure

c) Well, I'll go to the foot of our stairs

18. George's granddaughter told him that her new music teacher was 'flossin' in class. At the next parents' evening, why shouldn't George have been surprised when his conversation with the music teacher about the virtues of dental hygiene appeared to fall on stony ground?

19. Who might be encouraged to think outside the box?

    a) A magician

    b) An office worker

    c) A funeral director

20. In txt spk, does TBH stand for 'To Be Honest' or 'Terrible Bodily Harm', one step down from Grievous?

21. What would you be doing if you suddenly started twerking?

    a) Twitching

    b) Dancing in a suggestive manner

    c) Talking nonsense

22. Decline the future perfect tense of the verb 'to butt-dial'.

23. If you are 'owned' on social media, what has happened to you?

a) You have been purchased by mistake on eBay

b) You have been the subject of flattering comments

c) You have been made a fool of

24. What does 2MI stand for in text speak?

25. What name is given to a place specially created so that modern man can behave as he wishes with male friends – often in a somewhat unruly and debauched manner – without fear of incurring female disapproval?

a) Man cave

b) Golf club bar

c) Australia

26. George's granddaughter told him that the musical she went to see last week was 'sick'. Should he complain in the strongest possible terms to the theatre or realize that she was actually praising the production?

27. Is YOLO an abbreviation for 'You only live once' or 'You've eaten my last Rolo'?

28. A lowly paid neighbour of Sylvia needs hand-outs from the state to make ends meet. But why were Sylvia's husband and grown-up son alarmed when Sylvia loudly declared over Sunday lunch that she had a friend with benefits?

29.What is LOL an acronym for?

a) Lots Of Love

b) Laugh Out Loud

c) Lady Of Leisure

30. If your grandchildren tell you something is 'pants', do they mean ... ?

a) It is baggy

b) It is rubbish

c) It needs putting on a 50-degree wash cycle, whites only

31. Does the word 'chillax' mean to calm down and relax or to put your axe in the fridge before sharpening its blade?

32. If someone at work said 'Can I stir-fry an idea in your think-wok', what are they asking for?

a) Your recipe book

b) Your opinion

c) A right hook

33. George's granddaughter told him that she was 'flat roofin' for her GCSEs, but why was there no sign of any bitumen in her school satchel?

34. A pair of budgie smugglers might be convicted for a crime against what?

a) Ornithology

b) The stock market

c) Fashion

35. How many of these textspeak acronyms can you decipher, although you might wonder why you should need to?

a) BTDT

b) IFYP

c) MYOB

d) IMHO

e) POS

Answers on page 217

SECTION 4

You used to drink from the fountain of knowledge but now you just gargle and spit out. You struggle to keep up with modern technology to the point where you think Tumblr is a website for acrobats and a Twitter feed is a bird seed holder. You now avoid the Internet altogether following an unfortunate experience while searching for a knife sharpener on Grindr. Basically, you have failed to move with the times – in the Derby of life, you are a rocking horse. Your brain has spent too long in standby mode. Try and reboot it by answering these questions.

HISTORY

1. **Put these English kings in the order of their ascendancy to the throne: Henry IV, Henry III, Henry VI.**

2. **For what did Frederick William I, King of Prussia, have a particular fondness?**

   a) Cream buns

   b) Rabbits

   c) Giants

3. **Which of these is *not* a genuine patron saint?**

   a) St Louis – trumpet players

   b) St Valentine – beekeeping

   c) St Vitus – dancers

4. **True or false? The only matter on which Catholics and Protestants agreed in sixteenth-century England is that neither would open the door to Jehovah's Witnesses.**

5. What was the nickname of King Ethelred II, who ruled England in the tenth century?

a) The Underfed

b) The Unsteady

c) The Unready

6. What did the United States buy from Russia in 1867?

a) 20,000 fur hats

b) A consignment of Red Square snow globes

c) Alaska

7. Who beat Captain Scott to the South Pole?

a) Roald Dahl

b) Roald Amundsen

c) Ron Burgundy

8. What were nineteenth-century ladies travelling on trains advised to take with them in order to deter male passengers from attempting to kiss them in tunnels?

a) A hat pin

b) An alligator

c) A loaded rifle

9. From which World War I figure did the UK rock band Franz Ferdinand take their name?

a) Kaiser Wilhelm II of Germany

b) British Field Marshal Horatio Herbert Kitchener

c) Archduke Franz Ferdinand of Austria

10. Who became US president in 1829?

a) Andrew Jackson

b) Michael Jackson

c) Samuel L. Jackson

11. Which dynasty ruled China from 1368?

a) Ming

b) Qing

c) Carrington

12. The teddy bear was named after which US president?

a) Abraham Lincoln

b) George Washington

c) Theodore Roosevelt

13. True or false? Argentine revolutionary leader Che Guevara used to wind down by practising flower arranging.

14. What did the US buy from France for $15 million in 1803?

a) 150 million baguettes

b) 500 million cloves of garlic

c) 828,000 square miles of land

15. Which country did England fight in the Anglo-Dutch Wars of the seventeenth and eighteenth centuries?

16. Over what animal did Britain and the United States almost go to war in 1859?

a) Mule

b) Hamster

c) Pig

17. By what means of transport did Hannibal cross the Alps in 218 BC?

a) Pogo stick

b) Elephant

c) Roller skates

18. What did Englishman Howard Carter discover in 1922?

a) A blister on his big left toe

b) The secret of eternal youth

c) King Tutankhamun's tomb

19. Who was the leader of the Soviet Union from 1953 to 1964?

a) Nikita Khrushchev

b) Yuri Gagarin

c) Rudolf Nureyev

20. What was Julius Caesar warned to beware of shortly before his death?

a) Cold baths

b) The Ides of March

c) Roman double-glazing salesmen

21. According to legend, what inspired fourteenth-century Scottish king Robert the Bruce to defeat the English?

a) A spider

b) A wizened soothsayer

c) A self-help guide, *Ye Olde Booke of Mindfulnesse*

22. Which of these was *not* famous for having a little red book?

a) Mao Zedong

b) Richard Nixon

c) The Drifters

23. True or false? After losing his left leg in a battle with the French in 1838, Mexican general Antonio López de Santa Anna ordered the severed limb to be given a full state funeral.

24. What was the name of Queen Victoria's loyal Scottish personal servant?

a) John Brown

b) Billy Connolly

c) Kenneth McKellar

25. Which of these was not credited as being introduced to Britain by Sir Walter Raleigh?

a) Tobacco

b) The potato

c) The Chopper bike

26. The manufacture and sale of which commodity was banned in the US between 1920 and 1933?

a) Chewing gum

b) Alcohol

c) Cigars

27. True or false? Adolf Hitler once finished third in a Charlie Chaplin lookalike contest.

Answers on page 218

SCIENCE AND NATURE

1. What is unique about the kiwi?

   a) It is the only bird where the female's mating call is 'Stand By Your Man' by Tammy Wynette

   b) It is the only bird with nostrils at the tip of its beak

   c) It is the only bird to be a judge on *New Zealand's Got Talent*

2. Which of these does not swim in the ocean?

   a) Grey seal

   b) Leopard seal

   c) Royal seal

3. True or false? The Adelie penguin gets its name because they are all big fans of Adele.

4. George has Montezuma's revenge. Should he be taking ... ?

   a) Imodium

   or

   b) Senokot

5. What are only female mosquitoes able to do?

    a) Remember to put the toilet lid down

    b) Remember anniversaries

    c) Bite humans and drink their blood

6. Cats are conspicuous by their absence from which book?

    a) The Bible

    b) *The Bumper Book of Dogs*

    c) *Betty Crocker's Christmas Cookbook*

7. What is the name of the world's oldest living tortoise, thought to have turned 184 in 2016?

    a) Shelley

    b) Jonathan

    c) Michelle

8. True or false? The shark that is the most dangerous to humans is the loan shark.

9. If wood becomes fossilized, what is it described as?

    a) Scared

    b) Petrified

    c) Terrified

10. Is another name for a sea cow a manatee or a mannequin?

11. What do bats use to find their way around at night?

    a) Echo-location

    b) SatNav

    c) A good map

12. True or false? A cow in Iowa once 'flew' nearly half a mile after being sucked up by a tornado.

13. Which of these is the name of a family of small fish?

  a) Whift

  b) Smelt

  c) Stank

14. How does the clownfish gets its name?

  a) From its bright colours

  b) From its bulbous red nose

  c) From its ability to ride a unicycle backwards while sounding a horn

15. Sylvia was worried that her husband was becoming obese. Which of the following did she suggest he might need to have fitted around his stomach?

  a) An elastic band

  b) A gastric band

  c) A steel band

16. From which US state does the breed of chicken known as the Rhode Island Red originate?

17. For which of these did Louis Pasteur find a cure?

   a) Rabies

   b) Rabbis

   c) Rabbits

18. True or false? The funky gibbon
   officially became extinct in the wild in 1988.

19. What happens to a male praying mantis after sex?

   a) He lights a cigarette

   b) He falls asleep immediately and starts dreaming about
      football

   c) He often gets eaten by his partner

20. What essential item of mining equipment was invented
   by Sir Humphry Davy?

   a) The lunch box

   b) The safety lamp

   c) The pit pony

21. Does a mother kangaroo keep her young in a pouch or
   in a crèche?

22. The feathers from which species of duck were traditionally
   harvested for filling pillows and quilts?

   a) Eider duck

   b) Duvet duck

   c) Rubber duck

23. The proboscis monkey gets its name from its long what?

   a) Tail

   b) Nose

   c) Stories about other monkeys

24. Complete the animal in the title of this 1950s children's TV show: *Champion the Wonder ...*

a) *Skunk*

b) *Horse*

c) *Three-toed sloth*

25. Is a kittiwake a type of sea bird or a cat alarm?

26. Which one of these statements is true?

a) The puffin gets its name because it enjoys nothing more than sitting on cliff ledges smoking a pipe

b) An ostrich's eye is bigger than its brain

c) The albatross was named after a seventeenth-century explorer, Albert Ross

27. What did Hungarian Laszlo Biro invent?

a) The ballpoint pen

b) Half a pair of chopsticks

c) The super duper pooper scooper

28. True or false? Until 1818, there were no separately designed shoes for left and right feet.

29. Why are flamingos pink? Is it because ...

a) They eat a lot of shrimp

b) They blush a lot because they are easily embarrassed

c) They wear too much make-up

Answers on page 218

MATHS

1. George has four toffees in his pocket and then Alec gives him another five and Eric gives him another three. How long will it be before George has to go to the dentist?

2. How many times can you take 3 from 18?

3. Every month, Sylvia buys three ornamental gnomes at her local church sale. She currently has forty-five gnomes in her yard. How long has it taken her to build up her collection, and isn't it a shame she can't buy taste?

4. In geometry, what name is given to the longest side of a right-angled triangle?

   a) Hypothetical

   b) Hypotenuse

   c) Hippopotamus

5. How much would the Three Tenors have been worth in euros at an exchange rate of 1.20 to the pound?

6. True or false? Trigonometry is the study of Roy Rogers' horse.

7. George drinks a glass of wine every night – purely for medicinal reasons, of course. He gets six glasses out of a bottle, so how many bottles does he drink in a thirty-day month?

8. Is 7 squared ... ?

   a) 7

   b) 49

   c) 77

9. George has three doughnuts in one hand and two doughnuts in the other hand. How many doughnuts does he have in total, and is it any wonder he has to wear trousers with elasticated waistbands?

10. George has to phone his broadband provider's call centre. The first four minutes of his call are spent on security checks, confirming, re-confirming and re-re-confirming that he is the account holder and establishing how he would like to be addressed through the duration of the call. When he finally gets around to discussing the nature of his complaint, how much longer will it be before George longs for the good old days of the typewriter?

   a) Ten minutes

   b) Five minutes

   c) Less than two minutes

11. George opened the inbox on his laptop to find that he had received sixteen new emails. Three were from various gentlemen in Nigeria promising him thousands of dollars if he could just remind them of his bank details; two informed him that shapely young Russian women living nearby were just waiting for him to contact them; one said that for a modest monthly fee he could have a funeral to die for; one promised to increase his bra size in three weeks; one told him he had an urgent message from the FBI (probably about that overdue library book); two offered him the medication required to be hung like an elephant; one told him that he had inherited 60 million manat because a total stranger in Turkmenistan had left him a fortune in his will; one offered him discounted Botox for a month. Dismissing all of these as junk, how many emails did that leave that were actually worth reading?

Answers on page 218

THE ARTS

1. **Which popular duo split up in the 1970s over allegations of jealousy, after which they barely spoke to each other for several years?**

    a) Simon and Garfunkel

    b) Wham!

    c) Shari Lewis and Lamb Chop

2. **True or false? Meryl Streep based her portrayal of Margaret Thatcher in the film *The Iron Lady* on old videos of Arthur Askey playing Widow Twankey in *Aladdin*, the 1956 Christmas panto at the Sunderland Empire.**

3. **What TV reality show did Donald Trump once present?**

    a) *The Apprentice*

    b) *Say Yes to the Dress*

    c) *Pretty Wicked Moms*

4. **In what year was George Orwell's novel *Nineteen Eighty-Four* set?**

5. **What was the name of the dolphin that starred in a long-running TV series?**

    a) Flipper

    b) Philippa

    c) Norman

6. **What did pop band The Jacksons encourage you to blame it on in 1978?**

   a) Inflation

   b) The parents

   c) The boogie

7. **True or false? To prepare for his role in *Dances With Wolves*, Kevin Costner learned to do the Charleston with a team of huskies.**

8. **According to the title of the 2006 movie, what does the devil wear?**

   a) Gucci

   b) Prada

   c) Adidas

9. **What was the name of Starsky and Hutch's regular informant?**

   a) Rupert Bear

   b) Huggy Bear

   c) Fozzie Bear

10. **With which musical instrument is Charlie Parker most usually associated?**

    a) Triangle

    b) Saxophone

    c) Xylophone

11. **True or false? Nicki Minaj's three-girl backing group is called Minaj à Trois.**

12. **What is the name of the dragon in J. R. R. Tolkien's *The Hobbit*?**

    a) Smaug

    b) Deirdre

    c) Puff

13. Which of these was a fictional TV detective?

a) Frank Burns

b) Frank Cannon

c) Frank Sinatra

14. Which of these was the title of a 1973 Bruce Lee film?

a) *Enter the Dragon*

b) *Inter the Dragon*

c) *Carry On Nurse*

Hail, MᶜAnthony

15. True or false? Norway's entry for the 1980 Eurovision Song Contest was a song about the construction of a hydro-electric power plant.

16. Which Shakespeare play is often referred to simply as 'the Scottish play' for reasons of superstition?

a) *The Merchant of Venice*

b) *Julius Caesar*

c) *Macbeth*

17. In the title of their 1971 hit, soft rock trio America went through the desert on a horse with no ...

a) Name

b) Mane

c) Legs

18. Which fictional amateur sleuth was the heroine in a series of mystery fiction books written under the pseudonym Carolyn Keene?

a) Nancy Astor

b) Nancy Drew

c) Nancy Reagan

19. **True or false? Nineteenth-century French poet Gérard de Nerval used to take his pet lobster for walks on a leash along the Champs-Élysées in Paris.**

20. **Who sang the theme to Scott and Charlene's wedding in *Neighbours*?**

   a) Angry Anderson

   b) Irked Anderson

   c) Mildly Peeved Anderson

21. **According to a 2011 survey, 21 per cent of people believe which fictional character is a real person?**

   a) Sherlock Holmes

   b) Pinocchio

   c) Batman

22. **Was Ginger Rogers renowned for her tap dancing or her lap dancing?**

23. **David Gates was the chief singer-songwriter with which food-named band?**

   a) Black Eyed Peas

   b) The Raspberries

   c) Bread

24. **Which of these is an American singer-songwriter?**

   a) Richard Keys

   b) Alicia Keys

   c) Florida Keys

25. **Which two of these were not among Snow White's Seven Dwarfs?**

   a) Happy   d) Sleepy

   b) Grumpy   e) Sneezy

   c) Windy   f) Lanky

26. True or false? Harrison Ford psychs himself up for every film role by sitting in a corner of the studio with a cardboard box over his head.

27. What was the name of Popeye the Sailor Man's girlfriend?

a) Tugboat Annie

b) Olive Oyl

c) Penelope Pitstop

28. Who was the subject of the Don McLean song 'Vincent'?

a) Gene Vincent

b) Vincent Price

c) Vincent van Gogh

29. Which of these has never been a member of the Rolling Stones?

a) Ronnie Wood

b) Mick Taylor

c) Brian Jones

d) Joe 'Mr Piano' Henderson

30. True or false? The French playwright Molière died shortly after collapsing on stage while playing a hypochondriac in his own play *Le Malade imaginaire* (The Imaginary Invalid).

31. What is the battle call of *The Three Musketeers*?

a) 'All for one, one for all'

b) 'Once more unto the breach, dear friends'

c) 'Nice to see you, to see you nice'

Answers on page 219

FOOD AND DRINK

1. Which of these is a variety of cheese?

   a) Pungent Priest

   b) Stinking Bishop

   c) Mouldy Minister

   d) Dirty Deacon

   e) Rancid Reverend

2. The kiwifruit is also known as the Chinese what?

   a) Lantern

   b) Gooseberry

   c) Burn

3. What food are the Teenage Mutant Ninja Turtles addicted to?

   a) Pizza

   b) Caviar

   c) Brussels sprouts

4. True or false? Stilton cheese cannot legally be made in the Cambridgeshire village of Stilton where its name originated.

5. Why did the Pilgrim Fathers refuse to eat lobster?

   a) They were scared of getting too close to the claws

   b) They had forgotten to bring the garlic sauce

   c) They thought it was a giant insect

6. Which of these is a cut of beef?

   a) Brisket

   b) Friskit

   c) Riskit

7. If someone in Birmingham offered you canapés, would they be giving you a small piece of bread with a savoury topping or a tin containing small, round, green vegetables?

8. Which one of these has not yet been marketed as an ice cream flavour somewhere in the world?

   a) Crocodile egg

   b) Breast milk

   c) Coronation chicken

   d) Bacon

   e) Octopus

   f) Smoked salmon

   g) Cheeseburger

   h) Garlic

   i) Horsemeat

   j) Crispy rat

9. With what food is tartare sauce usually served?

   a) Meat

   b) Fish

   c) Doughnuts

10. True or false? If you like a full-bodied wine, China and Korea sell bottles of wine containing the corpses of fifteen dead baby mice.

11. Which of these is it considered socially acceptable to eat?

   a) Pomegranate

   or

   b) Pomeranian

12. Which of these is the name of a dish of chicken breast cooked around garlic butter?

   a) Chicken Kiev

   b) Chicken Riga

   c) Chicken Vladivostok

13. If a restaurant waiter offered you a 'digestif', would you expect to be given?

   a) A small alcoholic drink served after the meal

   or

   b) A biscuit covered on one side in chocolate

14. In which 1970s TV series did Hawkeye Pierce, played by Alan Alda, warn: 'I told you the food here should not be taken internally'?

15. Is ham hock ... ?

a) Pork in German white wine

b) Pork knuckle

c) Pork that is in debt

16. With which food is Winnie the Pooh most readily associated?

a) Marmalade

b) Honey

c) Milk of Magnesia

17. Which of these is a variety of tea?

a) Berry Sextet

b) Sir Douglas Quintet

c) Vienna Philharmonic Quartet

18. What do you traditionally put in a toaster?

a) Porridge

b) Bread

c) Soup

19. Which of these is a brand of rice?

a) Uncle Ben's

b) Gentle Ben's

c) Mr Benn's

20. True or false? Marmite yeast extract – a popular savoury spread on a slice of bread – was once considered to be an effective cure for beriberi and scrotal dermatitis.

21. What product is made by Lindt?

a) Chocolate

b) Champagne

c) Belly button fluff

22. Which of these is a measurement of beer?

a) Gherkin

b) Jerkin

c) Firkin

23. 'Once you pop, you can't stop' was an advertising slogan for which product?

a) Pringles

b) Bubble gum

c) Bubble wrap

24. What would you expect to find on a Hawaiian pizza?

a) Banana

b) Pineapple

c) An elephant

25. True or false? You grill a steak by interrogating it and asking it really difficult questions.

26. In Greek mythology, what was the food of the gods?

a) Ambrosia

b) Larks' tongues

c) A double Whopper with cheese

Answers on page 219

SPORT

1. The Great Kabuki, The Undertaker, Crybaby Cannon, Big Daddy and Giant Haystacks have all participated in which sport?

   a) Dressage

   b) Rhythmic Gymnastics

   c) Wrestling

2. Which American city stages the annual Indianapolis 500 motor race?

3. If your ball lands on an alligator at the Myakka Pines Golf Club in Florida, what do you get?

   a) A free drop

   b) A free holiday

   c) A new leg

4. Which of these was a leading racehorse jockey?

a) A. P. McCoy

b) 'Bones' McCoy

c) The Real McCoy

5. True or false? The Stoop, a stadium in south-west London, is the main venue in England for over-60s rugby.

6. What takes place each year at the Augusta National?

a) The Masters golf tournament

b) An annual redneck cull

c) The World Sock Darning Championships

7. Where might you experience a block, a scrimmage, a handoff, a smashmouth offense and a fumble?

a) On an American football field?

or

b) At the first day of the winter shopping mall sales

8. Which of these is not the title of a book about angling?

a) *The Compleat Angler*

b) *Fly Fishing*

c) *The Happy Hooker*

9. True or false? At the 2020 Olympics there is a plan to restrict the doubles tennis competition to doppelgängers only.

10. Which of these was a famous American baseball player?

a) Joe DiMaggio

b) Leonardo DiCaprio

c) Danny DeVito

11. Who said: 'Whenever I play golf with [former US president] Gerry Ford, I usually try to make it a foursome – Ford, me, a paramedic and a faith healer'?

a) Richard Nixon

b) Bob Hope

c) Edward Heath

12. If you see a jerk at the Olympics, are you … ?

a) Watching the weightlifting competition

or

b) Trying to get the man in front of you to sit down

13. What do competitors spit in the African sport of *bokdrol spoek*?

a) Cherry pits

b) Chewing gum

c) Kudu dung

14. Where was the 1991 Ryder Cup staged?

a) Treasure Island

b) Fantasy Island

c) Kiawah Island

15. True or false?
Dick Trickle was an American NASCAR driver who won more than 1,200 races.

16. How often are the Winter Olympic Games held?

a) Every two years

b) Every four years

c) Every time it snows

17. Which of these has never been a world heavyweight boxing champion?

a) Mike Tyson

b) Tyson Fury

c) Billy Fury

18. In which sport would you use a spider?

a) Fly fishing

or

b) Snooker

19. True or false? An American golfer once took 166 shots and two hours on a par-3 hole after her ball landed in a fast-flowing river and she rowed off downstream in pursuit of it.

20. By what name is Edson Arantes do Nascimento better known?

a) Pelé

b) Alan Shearer

c) Lulu

21. At which sport might you be thrown an aspirin?

a) Baseball

b) Boxing

c) Judo

22. Foxhunter helped secure a team gold medal for Britain at the 1952 Olympics. Was Foxhunter ... ?

a) A show-jumping horse

b) A greyhound

c) A racing pigeon

23. What was unusual about Ethiopian marathon runner Abebe Bikila, a double Olympic gold medallist in the 1960s?

a) He ran barefoot

b) He ran with his feet tied together

c) He ran backwards

24. George has bought tickets to watch the Sale Sharks. Will he be watching rugby union or extreme surfing?

25. Which of these is not a recognized position in competitive diving?

a) Pike

b) Tuck

c) Belly flop

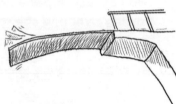

26. True or false? Play at the 1980 US Open Tennis Championships was suspended following an unsavoury incident on number two court at Flushing Meadows.

27. Which sporting event used to have a discipline called the 'clean and press'?

a) Weightlifting

or

b) Pro-celebrity washing

28. Which of these has managed in the English Premier League?

a) Dick Advocaat

b) Gerhard Pilsner

c) Roberto Martini

Answers on page 219

GEOGRAPHY

1. Spell Kyrgyzstan.

2. Which wall separates England from Scotland?

   a) Hadrian's Wall

   b) The Berlin Wall

   c) The Great Wall of China

3. True or false? The Scottish town of Fort William was named in honour of what King Harold did in 1066.

4. Which hat is traditionally associated with Mexicans?

   a) Trilby

   b) Sombrero

   c) Quaker bonnet

5. Is the international crime fighting organization that relies on co-operation between police forces of different countries known as Interpol or Interflora?

6. Which of these is a form of transport in some Asian countries?

a) Rickshaw

b) Chainsaw

c) Jigsaw

7. Which country is bordered by Peru, Brazil, Paraguay, Argentina and Chile?

a) Romania

b) India

c) Bolivia

8. According to recent figures, some 40,000 Americans have had themselves insured against what?

a) Stepping on a crack in the sidewalk and being eaten by bears

b) Finding a Great White Shark in the bath

c) Being kidnapped or eaten alive by aliens

9. Is the name of the French national anthem the Marseillaise or the Mayonnaise?

10. Alcatraz is an island in which bay?

a) Bay of Naples

b) San Francisco Bay

c) Bay of Biscay

11. What is the capital city of Belarus?

a) Mink

b) Musk

c) Minsk

12. True or false? The village of Dull in Scotland is twinned with the town of Boring in Oregon.

13. What does 'Bad' mean in front of German and Austrian town names?

a) It is a town with a high crime rate

b) It is a spa town

c) It is a town with a Michael Jackson tribute act

14. Which of these is an active volcano on the island of Sicily?

a) Mount Etna

b) Mount Edna

c) Mount Ada

15. Which of these world cities is the furthest south?

a) Stockholm

b) San Francisco

c) Cape Town

16. True or false? Due to fears that the original iron structure would corrode, the Eiffel Tower was dismantled in 1954 and rebuilt entirely with Lego.

17. What is the only country that has a border with Portugal?

a) France

b) Spain

c) China

18. Which Irish city floats on water?

19. Which of these is the name of a mountain range in Russia?

a) Murals

b) Urals

c) Urinals

20. Where would you find the Bull Ring shopping centre?

a) Valencia

b) Madrid

c) Birmingham

21. In which country would you find the Atacama Desert?

a) Switzerland

b) Chile

c) Scotland

22. What is the name of the peak overlooking Rio de Janeiro?

a) Meatloaf Mountain

b) Cheeseloaf Mountain

c) Sugarloaf Mountain

23. Which of these is a Canadian province?

a) New Hampshire

b) New Brunswick

c) New Mexico

Answers on page 219

WORDS

1. Is a small-bore ... ?

a) A type of firearm

or

b) Someone to avoid at parties

2. Is a catacomb ... ?

a) A device for grooming a pet's fur

or

b) An underground cemetery

3. What word can go before ache, pick and fairy?

4. Sylvia's brother wrote out a lonely hearts ad in which he described himself as an 'illegible bachelor'. Why didn't he get many replies?

5. Which country is known in its own language as 'Deutschland'?

a) Poland

b) Holland

c) Germany

6. True or false? 'Aromatic' is a word meaning autopilot for archers.

7. According to the proverb, the pen is mightier than the what?

   a) Pencil

   b) Sword

   c) Pigs

8. Which of these describes a creature that is half horse, half man?

   a) Centaur

   b) Centurion

   c) Senator

9. After his aunt died, Sylvia's brother filled out a death notice for the local newspaper in which he wrote that the old lady was 'recently diseased'. Why did the funeral director insist on writing all future notices himself?

10. What word can mean either a species of grey or red fish or a dubious haircut that is short at the front and sides and long at the back and was once popular with sportsmen and rock stars?

11. What is the wife of a sultan called?

   a) Currant

   b) Raisin

   c) Sultana

12. What word goes before jump, sleeved and John Silver?

13. Which of these is a type of small boat?

   a) Oracle

   b) Coracle

   c) Barnacle

14. What word describes a Hindu system of philosophic meditation designed to soothe mind and body?

   a) Yoga

   b) Toga

   c) Yogurt

15. What would you keep in an apiary – bees or apes?

16. Is Gorgonzola ... ?

   a) A Greek mythological woman with snakes for hair

   b) A blue-veined cheese

   c) A means of transport on canals in Venice

17. What name links O'Connor, Sutherland and Duck?

18. What is the French word for 'yes'?

   a) Si

   b) Oui

   c) Non

19. Is claustrophobia ...

   a) A fear of confined spaces

   or

   b) A fear of Santa Claus

20. Which of these is the name of a popular fairground ride?

a) Carousel

b) Casserole

c) Cassowary

21. The name of former German chancellor Helmut Kohl translates literally as what?

a) Helmut Leek

b) Helmut Broad Bean

c) Helmut Cabbage

22. Sylvia's brother said he wanted to earn shedloads of money so that he could be part of the 'effluent society'. Why does nobody take him seriously?

23. Which of these is not an anagram of 'rat'?

a) Art

b) Tar

c) Rhododendron

Answers on page 219

SECTION 5

Oh dear. Like a bad undertaker, you really have lost the plot. You've seen it all, you've done it all, but you can't remember most of it. You seem to walk around in a constant fog. People look at you and think: the wheel is still turning, but the hamster is dead. Last year, you forgot your sister's birthday – and she's your identical twin. So you decided to write down all important dates, names and passwords in a little book for safe keeping, which would be really helpful if only you could remember where you had put the book. You definitely have the feeling that you're past your sell-by date, so maybe these none-too-challenging questions will give you a welcome boost.

HISTORY

1. Who invented a new method of iron production during the Industrial Revolution?

a) Abraham Darby

b) Abraham Lincoln

c) Father Abraham and the Smurfs

2. Who was the first man to set foot on the moon?

a) Neil Diamond

b) Neil Armstrong

c) Neil Sedaka

3. True or false? Henry VIII employed a Groom of the Stool, whose job it was to wipe the king's bottom.

4. According to legend, the Pied Piper of Hamelin earned widespread praise for successfully luring all species of what away from the German town to meet their death by drowning in a nearby river?

a) Rat

b) Lawyer

c) Banker

5. Which soldier was famous for his Last Stand?

   a) Colonel Custer

   b) Colonel Sanders

   c) Major Roadworksahead

6. True or false? Five years after the mystery first came to light, it emerged that the crew of the *Mary Celeste* had merely been hiding.

7. Who was burned at the stake in the French city of Rouen in 1431?

   a) Joan of Arc

   or

   b) Noah of Ark

8. According to William Shakespeare, in a moment of desperation during the Battle of Bosworth, what was King Richard III of England prepared to sell his kingdom for?

   a) A horse

   b) A cigarette

   c) A Happy Meal

9. Who was the ancient Greek god of love?

   a) Viagra

   b) Eros

   c) Barry White

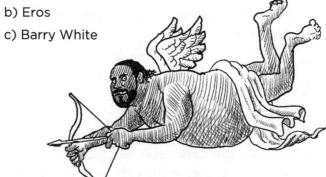

10. How did the Dark Ages, which started around the sixth century, get their name?

a) Because of the supposed cultural and economic deterioration that occurred in Western Europe following the fall of the Roman Empire

or

b) Because nobody could see where they were going as the Romans had forgotten to invent electricity

11. Which of these was a sixteenth-century ruler of the Ottoman Empire?

a) Suleiman the Magnificent

b) Suleiman the Adequate

c) Suleiman the Shi'ite

12. On which saint's day did the St. Valentine's Day Massacre take place in Chicago in 1929?

13. Who fiddled while Rome burned?

a) Yehudi Menuhin

b) Emperor Nero

c) Silvio Berlusconi

14. What was Christopher Columbus searching for when he discovered America?

a) His passport

b) His keys

c) India

15. True or false? William the Conqueror was elected leader of the Normans to avoid confusion because he was the only member of the invading army who was not called Norman.

16. On what did Norwegian explorer Thor Heyerdahl cross the Pacific Ocean in 1947?

a) Washing machine

b) Raft

c) Bicycle

17. What rather marred the performance of the play *Our American Cousin* at Ford's Theatre, Washington DC, on 14 April 1865?

a) The scenery collapsed, trapping the leading man beneath a polystyrene wall for ten minutes, during which he gamely continued to deliver his lines

b) The audience pelted the actors with eggs because they considered that the play was producing insufficient moments of merriment

c) President Lincoln was assassinated during Act Three

18. What was the name of King Arthur's queen?

a) Tracey

b) Guinevere

c) Jade

19. What threatened to sweep across Europe in 1588?

a) A huge Spanish Armada

or

b) A huge Spanish Armadillo

20. Which fearsome thirteenth-century Scottish warrior was the hero of the Mel Gibson movie *Braveheart*?

a) William Penn

b) William Wallace

c) William Shatner

21. True or false? Henry Hoover became president of the United States in 1929. The electorate said he sucked.

22. What did Cleopatra, Queen of Egypt, famously press to her bosom in the year 30 BC?

a) An asp

b) Mark Antony

c) A Playtex cross your heart bra

23. Where was Adolf Hitler's body found in 1945?

a) In a bunker

b) On the third tee

c) Out of bounds in some bushes

24. What does the United States Constitution grant to the people?

a) The right to bare arms

b) The right to bear arms

c) The right to arm bears

Answers on page 220

SCIENCE AND NATURE

1. Who invented television?

    a) John Logie Baird

    b) Yogi Bear

    c) Simon Cowell

2. Which of these is not a sea bird?

    a) Sooty Tern

    b) Fairy Tern

    c) Funny Tern

3. True or false? Lions in the Serengeti National Park in Tanzania congregate at their own exclusive watering-hole called the Lion Bar.

4. What animal represents Taurus in the Signs of the Zodiac?

a) Lion

b) Bull

c) Vole

5. Which of these is not a scientific law?

a) Boyle's Law

b) Cole's Law

c) Pascal's Law

6. What did Samuel Morse invent?

a) The unit of measure known as a morsel

or

b) Morse Code

7. True or false? The deaf leopard is a breed of big cat?

8. Which of these is not a breed of monkey?

a) Howler

b) Spider

c) Cheeky

9. What makes up the principal part of a giraffe's diet?

a) Spicy lamb vindaloo with pilau rice and naan bread

b) Chicken cacciatore in a red wine sauce with dauphinoise potatoes

c) Leaves

10. What colour is the African poisonous snake the green mamba?

a) Black

b) Brown

c) Green

11. True or false? Einstein's Theory of Relativity revealed the correct place on a family tree for second cousins.

12. Which nineteenth-century English mathematician is considered to be the 'Father of the Computer'?

a) Samuel Microsoft

b) Charles Babbage

c) Charles Cabbage

13. What is the main diet of an anteater?

14. Which one of these is not an approved alternative name for a dachshund?

a) Badger hound

b) Sausage dog

c) Draught excluder

15. True or false? The microwave oven was invented by Sir Frederick Microwave Oven, a 1940s entrepreneur.

16. Which of these is a species of lizard?

a) Prefect

b) Monitor

c) Head Girl

17. Which is larger – a hippopotamus or a pygmy hippopotamus?

18. Which of these is not a type of bee?

a) Honey bee

b) Bumble bee

c) Spelling bee

19. True or false? Yorkshireman Percy Shaw invented the cat's eye when, driving home one night, he saw a cat's eyes peering through the dark. He said that if the cat had been facing the other way he would have invented the pencil sharpener.

20. What is the name for a female deer?

a) Doe

b) Ray

c) Mee

21. Which of these is not a hoofed mammal or ungulate?

a) Camel

b) Alpaca

c) The Dalai Lama

22. True or false?

The woolly monkey can actually knit sweaters.

23. What type of tree can be destroyed by Dutch elm disease?

a) Oak

b) Ash

c) Sycamore

d) Yew

e) Maple

f) Plane

g) Willow

h) Horse chestnut

i) Sweet chestnut

j) Hazel

k) Poplar

l) Lime

m) Cherry

n) Douglas fir

o) Larch

p) Alder

q) Beech

r) Silver birch

s) Hornbeam

t) Juniper

u) Norwegian spruce

v) Maple

w) Giant redwood

x) Sequoia

y) Western red cedar

z) Elm

24. Which of these statements is true?

a) A little aardvark is called a cub

b) A little aardvark is called a leveret

c) A little aardvark never hurt anyone

Answers on page 220

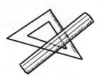

MATHS

1. Sylvia has three grandchildren. Child A works as a teacher and visits Sylvia regularly. Child B works as a nurse and visits Sylvia regularly. Child C works as an investment banker, makes a six-figure salary and never bothers to visit Sylvia. Which grandchild is Sylvia going to exclude from her will?

2. **How much soil is there in a hole 4 feet deep, 3 feet long and 2 feet wide?**

3. George and his wife go out to a restaurant for a meal. For his starter, George orders scallops while his wife chooses a cheese salad. He has four lovely scallops on his plate, but before he can begin eating them, his wife begs him for one. How many scallops does George have left to eat, and if his wife wanted them so badly, why didn't she order them, too, instead of cheese salad?

4. **Which of these is not a number divisible by 48?**

   a) 384

   b) 528

   c) A horse

5. **When replacing the toilet roll in the holder, George keeps forgetting that the paper should be positioned away from – and not next to – the wall. How many times has his wife reminded him about this over the past six months?**

   a) 1–10

   b) 10–20

   c) 20 or more

6. True or false? A logarithm is a lumberjack's chopping technique.

7. Lewis Hamilton drives recklessly around a small village in Lapland. Of the total population of fifty, he kills twenty villagers on the first circuit and another ten on the second. How many Lapps to go?

8. The builder has faithfully promised Sylvia that he will arrive at her house to start work on her extension at 8.30 in the morning – on the dot, without fail, 100 per cent guaranteed. At roughly what time should she really expect him?

Answers on page 220

THE ARTS

1. Who succeeded Sean Connery as suave secret agent James Bond?

a) Roger Moore

b) Dudley Moore

c) Patrick Moore

2. Which of these acts found fame on the TV talent show *Opportunity Knocks*?

a) Pink Floyd

b) Lena Zavaroni

c) Wolfgang Amadeus Mozart

3. Whose 2004 autobiography was titled *My Life* by Bill Clinton?

4. Who was Barney Rubble's best friend?

a) Oliver Stone

b) Fred Flintstone

c) Sharon Stone

5. In the band's original line-up, which three members of the Beach Boys were brothers?

a) Carl Wilson

b) Brian Wilson

c) Mike Love

d) Dennis Wilson

e) Al Jardine

6. Which of these was not a movie sequel?

a) *Back to the Future 2*

b) *Rocky 2*

c) *Mange 2*

7. True or false? 'Stairlift to Heaven' is the title of an epic Led Zeppelin track.

8. In the TV series *Downton Abbey*, who is the eldest daughter of the Earl of Grantham?

a) Lady Mary

b) Lady Marmalade

c) Lady Gaga

9. Which of these is not necessarily a musical instrument?

a) French horn

b) Flugelhorn

c) Shoe horn

10. Which of these is the title of a 2012 novel by John Green?

a) *The Fault in Our Stars*

or

b) *The Fault in Our Stairs*

11. According to Joni Mitchell's song 'Big Yellow Taxi', what did they pave in order to put up a parking lot?

a) The rose bed in her front garden

b) Paradise

c) The town cemetery

12. Which of the following has never won an Academy Award for Best Actress?

a) Bette Davis

b) Vivien Leigh

c) Joan Crawford

d) Ingrid Bergman

e) Katharine Hepburn

f) Miss Piggy

g) Meryl Streep

h) Jodie Foster

13. Which of these is a popular dance originating in the Dominican Republic?

a) Merengue

b) Meringue

c) Orang-utan

14. True or false? The first dog to play Rin Tin Tin in a movie was not a real German Shepherd but two Yorkshire terriers stitched together.

15. What was the name of Buddy Holly's backing band?

a) The Locusts

b) The Crickets

c) The Rhinoceros Beetles

16. Which of these was not a loveable character in *The Wind in the Willows*?

a) Ratty

b) Mole

c) Pterodactyl

17. Whose voice is higher?

a) A baritone

b) A tenor

c) A man in bare feet who has accidentally stepped on an upturned three-pin plug

18. What is the name of the 6 feet, 3 inch-tall invisible rabbit in Mary Chase's stage play?

a) Thumper

b) Roger

c) Harvey

19. Which US rock band was named after the dog from *The Wizard of Oz*?

a) Toto

b) Aerosmith

c) Alice Cooper

20. True or false? *Breakfast at Tiffany's* was to have been titled *Breakfast at Wendy's* but the US fast food chain refused permission for its name to be used.

21. Which current Hollywood actress was named after *Gone with the Wind* heroine Scarlett O'Hara?

a) Megan Fox

b) Scarlett Johansson

c) Vanessa Hudgens

22. Which of these was not a character in the *Mr Men* books by Roger Hargreaves?

a) Mr Chatterbox

b) Mr Nosey

c) Little Miss Psychopath

23. What breed of dog was the fearsome hound in the Sherlock Holmes adventure *The Hound of the Baskervilles*?

a) Toy poodle

b) Great Dane

c) Chihuahua

24. Complete the title of this Shakespeare play: *The Merry Wives of ...*

a) Orange County

b) Henry VIII

c) Windsor

25. True or false? It is bad luck to say 'Break a leg' to an actor who is about to go on stage, and for them then to fall over in the wings and break a leg.

26. Which of these films did not feature a killer shark?

a) *Jaws*

b) *Jaws 2*

c) *Pride and Prejudice*

27. Who starred as Batman in the 2016 movie *Batman v Superman: Dawn of Justice*?

a) Ben Affleck

b) Ben Hur

c) Ben Nevis

28. Which of these is not the title of a Harry Potter book?

a) *Harry Potter and the Philosopher's Stone*

b) *Harry Potter and the Order of the Phoenix*

c) *Harry Potter and the Lost Spectacles (I Know They're Here Somewhere)*

29. George likes to play the accordion, whether anyone asks him to or not. At what distance is the sound of the accordion best appreciated?

a) One mile

b) Two miles

c) Five miles

Answers on page 220

FOOD AND DRINK

1. Which of these is not an ingredient of chocolate mousse?

   a) Chocolate

   b) Eggs

   c) Moose

2. True or false? To prepare a chicken for the oven, top chefs say: 'Chicken, you're going in the oven.'

3. Which of these is a type of red wine?

   a) Bête Noire

   b) Pinot Noir

   c) Film Noir

4. Which of these makes ice cream?

a) Ben & Jerry's

b) Tom & Jerry's

c) Mork & Mindy's

5. If you fillet a fish, what do you do to it?

a) Remove all the bones and use it as a glove puppet

b) Remove all the bones without using it as a glove puppet

c) Teach it to dance the Argentine tango

6. Pontefract cakes are named after which town in Yorkshire?

a) Harrogate

b) Thirsk

c) Pontefract

7. True or false? Gravlax is a leading brand of laxative for salmon.

8. Which part of a horse do they not eat in France?

a) Withers

b) Loins

c) Shoulder

d) Saddle

9. What food do you usually put in an egg cup?

10. What is the national dish of Austria?

a) Wiener schnitzel

or

b) Lederhosen

11. Which of these ingredients would you expect to find in a shepherd's pie?

a) Creamy mashed potato

b) Minced beef or lamb

c) The tenderest cuts from the rump of an organically reared, free-range, locally sourced, eco-friendly shepherd

12. If you dress a crab, do you?

a) Clean it in readiness for cooking

or

b) Put it in a nice gown with matching pearls

13. Which of these is not a variety of rice?

a) Basmati rice

b) Lemon rice

c) Condoleezza Rice

14. True or false? Buffalo wings come from a little known breed of Argentine flying cow.

15. Which of these is not a chocolate manufacturer?

a) Cadbury

b) Nestlé

c) Black & Decker

16. What three ingredients would you expect to see in a BLT sandwich?

a) Bacon, lettuce and tomato

b) Beetroot, lemon and turnip

c) Badger, locust and tarantula

17. Is a celery stalker ... ?

a) Someone who cleans and trims celery ready for consumption

or

b) Someone who harasses and intimidates celery by following it around day and night

18. Which of these should you refrain from eating?

a) Hot dog

b) Corn dog

c) Sausage dog

19. True or false? The Waldorf Salad was named after New York's Hilton Hotel.

20. Which of these is a popular brand of US whisky?

a) Jack Daniel's

b) Jack Sparrow's

c) Jack Nicholson's

21. Which of these is a traditional Italian dessert?

a) Pikachu

b) Tiramisu

c) Coypu

22. If food is cooked so that it is firm 'to the teeth', is the correct culinary term ... ?

a) Al dente

b) Alfresco

c) Alcapone

23. Which Australasian dessert was created in honour of a famous dancer?

a) The Ginger Rogers Soufflé

b) The Gene Kelly Flapjack

c) Pavlova

24. Which of these might you be surprised to find on your plate at a restaurant?

a) Asparagus spears

b) Broccoli spears

c) Britney Spears

Answers on page 221

SPORT

1. Who ran the 100 metres in 9.63 seconds to win gold at the 2012 Olympic Games?

a) Usain Bolt

b) Queen Beatrix of the Netherlands

c) A haddock

2. Which of these won the men's singles final at Wimbledon on three separate occasions?

a) Boris Johnson

b) Boris Karloff

c) Boris Becker

3. In the four-man bob event at the Winter Olympics, would you expect to see four men racing in a bobsleigh or just four men called Bob?

4. If you perform a 'deadlift' in international competition, are you most likely ... ?

a) A weightlifter at the Olympics

or

b) An undertaker at the World Funeral Games

5. Which golfer is nicknamed 'Big Phil'?

a) Ben Crenshaw

b) Paul Azinger

c) Phil Mickelson

6. True or false? Mo Farah prepared for the 2016 Olympics by bouncing on a Spacehopper to the summit of Mount Snowdon.

7. Does a strike in bowling mean?

    a) All 10 pins have been knocked down with one ball

    or

    b) The alley is closed due to industrial action

8. Which city hosted the 2016 United States Formula One Grand Prix?

    a) Austin, Texas

    b) Austin, Texas

    c) Austin, Texas

9. Who was the Argentine footballer who was named FIFA World Player of the Year at the age of twenty-two?

    a) Lionel Messi

    or

    b) Lionel Richie

10. Are 'prop forward' and 'line out' terms used in ... ?

    a) Rugby union

    or

    b) Hanging out the washing

11. Which of these never won the Formula One world drivers' championship?

    a) Graham Hill

    b) Damon Hill

    c) Harry Hill

12. True or false? Pool players regularly need a 'rest' because the game is so physically demanding.

13. If you rode a skeleton, would you most likely be ... ?

a) Lying face down on a sled and hurtling down a frozen track in the name of sport

or

b) Banned for life from the Natural History Museum

14. Which of these was a major American basketball star with the Chicago Bulls and the Washington Wizards?

a) Michael Jordan

or

b) King Hussein of Jordan

15. Jockey Greville Starkey was associated with riding what kind of animal?

a) Racehorse

b) Camel

c) Greyhound

16. In total, how many players are on the court at the same time in a game of doubles tennis?

a) 2

b) 4

c) 76

17. True or false? In real life, bishops may only move diagonally, just as they do in chess.

18. In which sport does the leader wear the yellow jersey? Is it?

a) Cycling

or

b) Egg throwing

19. Which of the following terms would a competitor least want to hear during a sailing race?

a) Prepare to jibe!

b) Jibe-ho!

c) Abandon ship!

20. If a sportsman performs a 'full nelson' does he ... ?

a) Carry out a wrestling move

or

b) Chop off his right arm and engage in naval combat with the French

21. Which of these is not an Alpine skiing discipline?

a) Downhill

b) Super-G

c) Nana Mouskouri

22. Which of these has been crowned world snooker champion?

a) Ronnie Barker

b) Ronnie O'Sullivan

c) Peter O'Sullevan

23. Is a 'bully' in field hockey … ?

a) The name for the set play that is used to restart the game

or

b) Someone with a bigger stick than everyone else

24. True or false? Knitting was an Olympic sport until 1928 when three members of the Albanian team were banned on suspicion of taking drugs after used needles were discovered on the team bus.

25. Which of these is a titanic challenge of strength and endurance?

a) Iron Man

b) Hoover Man

c) Doing the Dishes Man

26. How does a game of ice hockey start?

a) Face-off

b) Lift-off

c) Clothes off

Answers on page 221

GEOGRAPHY

1. When the first convicts were transported from England in the late eighteenth century, where in Australia did they arrive?

a) Botany Bay

b) Biology Bay

c) Scientology Bay

2. North Island is the name of one of the two islands that make up New Zealand. What is the name of the other island? Concentrate ...

3. Which river flows into the sea near Buenos Aires?

a) River Saucer

b) River Plate

c) River Phoenix

4. Which of these is not a city in Belgium?

a) Ghent

b) Genk

c) Madrid

5. Which one of these statements is true?

a) A remote tribe in Papua New Guinea has adopted Paris Hilton as its spiritual leader

b) The Pyramids in Egypt don't really exist: they are just a mirage

c) Rome is the capital of Italy

6. Which of these is not a British royal residence?

a) Windsor Castle

b) Balmoral Castle

c) Elephant and Castle

7. According to legend, what should you kiss when visiting Blarney Castle in Ireland?

a) The Blarney Stone

b) The bottom of the person standing in front of you

c) The little old lady in the castle gift shop

8. In which country would you find the Costa del Sol?

a) Spain

or

b) Scotland

9. Which of these is not the name of a Japanese island?

a) Honshu

b) Kyushu

c) Pingu

10. True or false? The Lost City of Atlantis has recently been discovered in storage in a warehouse near Peterborough.

11. What is the name of the major opera house in Sydney, Australia?

a) The Taj Mahal

b) The Empire State Building

c) The Sydney Opera House

12. How do Eskimos traditionally greet each other?

a) With a hearty song

b) By rubbing noses

c) By playfully slapping each other around the face with a dead mackerel

13. Which Australian city is named after a famous scientist?

a) Darwin

b) Brisbane

c) Alice Springs

14. Where does the Pope live?

a) In the Vatican

b) In a vacuum

c) Detroit

15. When Sylvia visited Japan, she found that the traditional native garment she was given was a bit too long for her. Did her host say that Sylvia had a kimono draggin' or a Komodo dragon?

16. Which of these is not an Australian state?

a) South Australia

b) Western Australia

c) Texas

17. The English Channel separates England from which other country?

a) Scotland

b) France

c) Australia

18. Which river flows through London?

a) Nile

b) Amazon

c) Thames

19. True or false? The Dalmatian coast in Croatia gets its name because all of the inhabitants suffer from severe acne.

20. Which of these is not the name of a Greek island?

a) Zakinthos

b) Mikonos

c) Domestos

21. Denmark, Sweden, Norway, Finland and Iceland make up which group of countries?

a) Central America

b) Scandinavia

c) Australasia

22. Which of these is the name of one of the Great Lakes of North America?

a) Erie

b) Spookie

c) Creepie

23. According to superstition, on both sides of the Atlantic what is it considered bad luck to walk under?

a) A ladder

or

b) A black cat

24. What is the capital of South Korea?

a) Motown

b) Disco

c) Seoul

25. Which stretch of water separates Japan from mainland Asia?

a) Gulf of Mexico

b) Arctic Ocean

c) Sea of Japan

Answers on page 221

WORDS

1. Which of these is another name for a tyrannical ruler?

   a) Despot

   b) Tosspot

   c) Cesspit

2. What preposition is an anagram of 'no'? Take your time ...

3. Which of these is not the name for a family member?

   a) Stepmother

   b) Stepfather

   c) Stepladder

4. When Sylvia's brother told her that his new job was easy money and that he felt like he had finally jumped on the gravy boat, why did she shake her head in despair?

5. True or false? 'Impolite' is the word used to describe a burning elf.

6. If an American describes someone as a 'regular guy', does it mean he … ?

a) Has a 32-inch inside leg measurement

b) Is humble and decent

c) Eats All-Bran twice a day

7. If a house is 'gutted', is it extremely upset or burnt to the ground?

8. If someone crosses your palm with silver, would you expect?

a) To be handed money

or

b) To be trodden on by the Lone Ranger's horse

9. How many 'i's are there in 'Mississippi'? (You may need your reading glasses for this question.)

10. After booking a restaurant, Sylvia told her brother that they would 'go Dutch' on dinner. Why was she surprised when he turned up wearing clogs?

11. What word do you associate with reaching the age of sixty?

a) Milestone

b) Millstone

c) Gallstone

12. Which is the odd one out?

a) An egg

b) A carpet

c) A nice cup of tea

13. Is having one wife?

   a) Monogamy

   or

   b) Monotony

14. George's wastrel son was unable to account for his whereabouts when some cash was stolen from his office. So before being questioned by the police, what did he ask George for?

   a) A wallaby

   b) A lullaby

   c) An alibi

15. Are 'polaroids' instant photographs or what Eskimos get from sitting on the ice too long?

16. According to the saying, too many cooks spoil what?

   a) Their grandchildren

   b) The broth

   c) Daytime television

17. Does the Latin phrase _bona fide_ mean 'genuine' or 'good dog'?

18. Sylvia's sister said she didn't trust her boss because he was just a 'wolf in cheap clothing'. How should she have phrased it?

19. Does the word 'illegal' refer to something that is unlawful or a sick bird of prey?

20. Which of these is the name of an international crime organization, operating originally in Sicily?

a) The mafia

or

b) The raffia

21. If someone handed you a baklava, would you?

a) Put it on your head and attempt to rob a bank

or

b) Eat it for dessert

22. On a family trip to Paris, Sylvia's hungry brother said he was going out to 'look for a nice brassiere' and hoped he might find one with room for four. What word should he have used to describe the type of establishment that would have better satisfied his appetite?

23. In the words of the proverb, what should people in glasshouses not do?

a) Throw stones

b) Throw orgies

24. Sylvia's brother said that what he really fancies for his old age is 'one of those Ladyboy recliners'. What did he mean to say, and is this why his family have banned him from ever visiting Bangkok?

25. On a ship, is the poop deck ...

a) The deck that forms the roof of a cabin in the rear of the vessel

or

b) The deck that the sailors use when the washroom is busy

26. When you toast the bride and groom at a wedding, do you ... ?

a) Raise a glass to their future happiness

or

b) Forcibly hold them over a bed of hot burning coals

27. What word goes before 'Valentino' and 'the Red-Nosed Reindeer'?

Answers on page 221

ANSWERS

SECTION 1

History
1.b 2.c 3.b 4.b 5.c 6.False 7.b 8.Franklin D. Roosevelt 9.c
10.c 11.Lady Jane Grey 12.b 13.Berwick-upon-Tweed 14.c
15.True 16.a 17.Anne of Cleves 18.b 19.True 20.b 21.c 22.a
23.c 24.True 25.c – he bestowed the title upon himself.
26.c

Science and Nature
1.b 2.b 3.False 4.a 5.a 6.Cloud 7.b 8.b 9.b 10.True 11.c 12.c
13.Bull 14.b 15.c 16.c 17.True 18.a 19.Viper 20.c 21.True
22.b 23.b 24.a 25.b 26.c

Maths
1.Nine minutes 2.Seventy 3.fifty-seven days 4.Technically
false 5. Thirty weeks 6.Thirty-six 7.3:1 8.Four 9.121
10.George would take 197 minutes and the paramedics
would take twenty-two minutes. 11.Eleven 12.252

The Arts
1.b 2.b 3.Michael Crichton 4.c 5.True 6.c 7.c 8.a 9.'I am
serious ... and don't call me Shirley.' 10.a 11.c 12.Margaret
Mitchell 13.b 14.b 15.He is the only member of the band

without a beard 16.b 17.True 18.c 19.b 20.Rip Van Winkle
21.b 22.False 23.a 24.c 25.Peter Parker 26.c 27.True 28.a
29.The Who 30.c 31.William Shakespeare 32.b 33.Flea
34.b

Food and Drink

1.b 2.c 3.True. You are much more likely to be killed by
a vending machine than by a shark (especially on dry
land), although actual attacks by vending machines
are rarer. 4.c 5.Belgium 6.b 7.c 8.False, although boiled
gannet meat is considered a tasty delicacy on the
Western Isles. 9.b 10.a 11.Make mash – it is a variety of
potato. 12.a 13.b 14.True 15.b 16.Lettuce 17.a 18.b 19.b
20.a 21.b 22.c 23.a 24.c

Sport

1.c 2.c 3.Chicago 4.False 5.b 6.b 7.c 8.a 9.Primo Carnera
10.c 11.True 12.b 13.c 14.Joe Frazier 15.c. – America had
forgotten that Greece still used the old Julian calendar,
which was eleven days in advance. 16.b 17.Basketball
18.b 19.Bob Beamon 20.c 21.c 22.True 23.a 24.b
25.Switzerland 26.a 27.b 28.American football 29.a
30. Michael Holding 31.b

Geography

1.b 2.Indiana 3.a 4.True 5.c 6.c 7.Alabama, Alaska,
Arizona, Idaho, Indiana, Iowa, Ohio, Oklahoma 8.a 9.a
10.True 11. Italy c 12.b 13.True – for use in fertilizer. 14.b
15.b 16.Belize 17.c 18.c 19.c 20.b 21.b 22.False, although
it has probably happened on stag and hen nights or
indeed any Saturday night. 23.c 24.Ontario 25.b 26.a
27.Ecuador, Colombia and Brazil 28.d and g – Mauritius
and Nicobar are both in the Indian Ocean. 29.b

Words

1.b 2.c 3.True 4.a 5.Ear 6.c 7.b 8.Honey 9.b 10.c 11.Beer 12.b 13.b 14.Stool 15.a 16.An armpit 17.c 18.False 19.b 20.He wanted a palette – if they had bought him a new palate, he would have received a new roof for his mouth, and they're not easy to come by, even on Amazon. 21.Stock 22.c 23.Cobbler 24.c 25.c

SECTION 2

History

1.b 2.b 3.George III 4.c 5.c 6.True 7.c 8.The Royalists or Cavaliers 9.a 10.b 11.a 12.fourteenth 13.a 14.b 15.False 16.a 17.a 18.c 19.a 20.John Adams 21.b 22.a 23.a 24.False – he was a minor, being under the required age to rule alone. He was nine when he was crowned and died six years later, never once venturing down a pit in his short life. 25.c 26.a 27.b 28.Ferdinand Magellan 29.a 30.c 31.b 32.b 33.True 34.b 35.a 36.b 37.True 38.b – Ming the Merciless is the villain in *Flash Gordon* and Conan the Barbarian is a fictional hero created by Robert E. Howard in 1932; Vlad the Impaler, who ruled modern-day southern Romania in the fifteenth century, was the real-life inspiration for Count Dracula.

Science and Nature

1.b 2.True 3.b 4.a 5.b 6.Honesty 7.b 8.b 9.True 10.a 11.b 12.A climbing plant 13.b 14.a 15.False, if only because they haven't thought of it yet. 16.b – because of an unusually shaped larynx it produces a yodel-like sound called a 'baroo'. 17.c 18.b 19.b 20.Perch 21.c 22.b 23.True 24.b 25.b

Maths

1.Fifteen 2.Sixty-eight 3.Fifty-two 4.Twenty minutes
(in theory) 5.120 minutes (two hours) 6.3,020 yards
7.Fifty minutes 8.Twelve 9.Three hours and five
minutes 10.Never – the boat rises along with the water.
11.Twenty-four minutes 12.Eighty-four 13.One-fifth
14.Twelve 15.Eighty per cent – and about two.

The Arts

1. c 2.c 3.b 4.c 5.b 6.False – Eric Clapton is his real name.
7.b 8.a 9.a 10.Joan Hickson 11.b 12.a 13.c 14.Volkswagen
Beetle 15.b 16.d 17.a 18.Davy Crockett 19.a 20.a 21.b 22.a
23.c 24.False – well, it never made the papers. 25.c 26.b
27.Ruby 28.b 29.a 30.c 31.True 32.a 33.a 34.Clark Gable
35.a 36.b 37.a 38.True 39.c

Food and Drink

1.c 2.a 3.b 4.False – sadly 5.a 6.b 7.a 8.c – Fellini was a
composer. 9.c 10.Burgundy 11.c 12.a 13.b 14.b 15.True 16.b
17.c – Glen Matlock was a member of the Sex Pistols.
18.b 19.Mateus 20.b 21.a 22.False 23.c 24.a 25.c

Sport

1.b 2.a 3.a 4.True 5.b 6.b 7.c 8.b 9.b 10.a 11.a 12.b 13.Eldrick
14.b 15.a 16.c 17.Golf – they're all in the US. 18.False –
Henry Cooper's twin was George, who boxed as Jim!
19.a 20.c 21.Chukka 22.b 23.Dennis Rodman 24.c 25.True
– he lost his real ear in a 1955 crash when it was sliced
off by his goggles and was given a plastic replacement
by doctors. He kept the spare plastic ear in case the
replacement one fell off and also to amuse fans. 26.a 27.a
28.b 29.b 30.a 31.John McEnroe 32.a)Rome b)Buenos
Aires c)London d)San Sebastián e)Turin f)Moscow

Geography

1.c 2.b 3.False 4.a 5.Paisley 6.c 7.True 8.b 9.a 10.b
11.Missouri 12.c 13.b 14.True 15.a 16.Limerick 17.c 18.a
19.Afghanistan and Azerbaijan 20.b 21.b 22.c 23.False
24.b 25.b 26.b 27.b

Words

1.a 2.Table 3.b 4.a 5.Club 6.c 7.False 8.b 9.Base 10.c
11.An antidote – unless you think the pain will be taken
away by hearing a long story. 12.b 13.Electric 14.c 15.a
16.Balmy – unless it was crazy weather, in which case
it could be barmy, too. 17.a 18.b 19.True 20.c 21.b 22.He
meant 'figment' of her imagination. 23.a – preferably,
because it is Australian slang for a bush toilet. 24.Peter
25.Abscess 26.a 27.He meant to say he had a 'deprived'
childhood. 'Depraved' would suggest it was immoral
and perverted.

SECTION 3

History

1.a 2.b 3.a 4.Ian Smith 5.b 6.c 7.False 8.a 9.George W.
Bush 10.b 11.a 12.b 13.True 14.b 15.b 16.Jimmy Carter 17.a
18.b 19.b 20.False 21.c 22.a 23.Agincourt 24.c 25.a 26.a
27.Pierre Trudeau 28.a 29.a 30.b

Science and Nature

1.a 2.True 3.b 4.f 5.Overweight 6.a 7.False 8.c 9.a 10.True
11.b 12.Pluto 13.c 14.c 15.True 16.a 17.b 18.c 19.c 20.c
21.False – probably 22.b 23.b

Maths

1.Thirty-three 2.12.7Mb 3.All of them. 4.Forty per cent 5.Twenty-two 6.None – the rapper 50 Cent wasn't in the band Dollar; it was Thereza Bazar and David Van Day. 7.1.5 million 8.*Five Shades of Grey* 9.Nineteen 10.Thirty-six 11.Fifty-eight 12.Twenty-eight bottles, seventy shots and about 5 per cent.

The Arts

1.b 2.b 3.b 4.False 5.a 6.Pink 7.c 8.a)Beliebers b)Swifties c)KatyCats 9.b 10.b 11.*Slumdog Millionaire* 12.b 13.c 14.False 15.a 16.a 17.c 18.a 19.a 20.INXS 21.a 22.a 23.a 24.b 25.b 26.b 27.False 28.a 29.b 30.False – as far as anyone knows. 31.b 32.c 33.a 34.c 35.c 36.False, although a different Ricky Martin did win the UK version of *The Apprentice* that year. 37.b 38.b 39.e 40. Kim, Kourtney, Khloé, Kendall and Kylie (the last two have the surname Jenner and are half-sisters to the Kardashians). So now you know. All you need to do now is care. 41.Little Mix, Dido, Justin Timberlake, Foo Fighters, Mary J. Blige, R Kelly.

Food and Drink

1.c 2.True 3.b 4.Mussels 5.b 6.True 7.b 8.c 9.a 10.Pepperoni 11.b 12.True 13.e 14.b 15.a 16.Australia 17.a 18.c 19.b 20.b 21.False 22.a 23.b 24.c 25.c – a Nebuchadnezzar is equivalent to twenty standard bottles, a Methuselah is eight and a Jeroboam is four. A Melchizedek is the biggest of all, equivalent to forty standard bottles. 26.True 27.a 28.c

Sport

1.b 2.b 3.c 4.c 5.a 6.c 7.False 8.a 9.c 10.c 11.a 12.b 13.five 14.b 15.c 16.b 17.b 18.True 19.c 20.c 21.b 22.False 23.b 24.a 25.a 26.b 27.b 28.b

Geography

1.b 2.b 3.b 4.True 5.c 6.b 7.California, Connecticut, Georgia, Iowa, Kentucky, Maine, Maryland, New Hampshire, New York, Oklahoma, Vermont and Wisconsin. 8.b 9.Bermuda 10.a 11.b 12.A town in Michigan 13.a 14.b 15.b 16.c 17.b 18.b 19.c 20.True 21.d 22.Chad, Mali and Togo 23.b

Words

1.b 2.A middle manager 3.b 4.A stylish, cultured man 5.c 6.b 7.None – it means 'cool'. 8.a 9.a 10.Bromance 11.b 12.Totally 13.c 14.Old-fashioned media 15.In today's vocabulary, a 'keeper' means a partner worth keeping. 16.False 17.b 18.'Flossin' is one of the dozens of modern slang words that mean 'awesome'. 19.b 20.To Be Honest 21.b 22.I shall have butt-dialled, You (singular) will have butt-dialled, He/She will have butt-dialled, We will have butt-dialled, You (plural) will have butt-dialled, They will have butt-dialled. 23.c 24.Too Much Information 25.a 26.'Sick' is now a term of praise, meaning 'cool' or 'awesome'. 27.You only live once. 28.'Friends with benefits' are friends who have no-strings sex with each other without being in a relationship. 29.b 30.b 31.Calm down and relax 32.b 33.'Flat roofin' is slang for 'working flat out'. 34.c –They are brief, tight-fitting men's swimming trunks. 35.a)Been There, Done That b)I Feel Your Pain c)Mind Your Own Business d)In My Humble Opinion e)Parents Over Shoulder.

History

1. Henry III, Henry IV, Henry VI 2.c – Soldiers in his army were all over 6 feet tall, and he even resorted to kidnapping tall people from other European countries. 3.a 4.False – but only because Jehovah's Witnesses weren't around in spirit until the late nineteenth century and not by name until 1931. 5.c 6.c 7.b 8.a 9.c 10.a 11.a 12.c 13.False 14.c – it was the Louisiana Purchase. 15.The Netherlands 16.c. The so-called Pig War started with the shooting of a pig, but there was no further bloodshed during the thirteen-year confrontation. 17.b 18.c 19.a 20.b 21.a 22.b 23.True 24.a 25.c 26.b 27.False

Science and Nature

1.b 2.c The royal seal is used for authenticating documents. 3.False 4.a – he has a bad case of diarrhoea. 5.c 6.a 7.b 8.True – more people suffer each year as a result of debt than are attacked by sharks. 9.b 10.Manatee 11.a 12.True 13.b 14.a 15.b 16.Er, Rhode Island 17.a 18.False 19.c 20.b 21.Pouch 22.a 23.b 24.b 25.Sea bird 26.b 27.a 28.True 29.a

Maths

1. At that daily rate of consumption, probably two weeks. 2.Only once, because after you take the first 3 away, it is no longer 18. 3.Fifteen months 4.b 5.36 euros 6.False – it is a branch of mathematics 7.Five 8.b 9.Five 10.c 11.Four

The Arts

1.a 2.False 3.a 4.1984 5.a 6.c 7.False 8.b 9.b 10.b 11.False 12.a 13.b 14.a 15.True 16.c 17.a 18.b 19.True 20.a 21.a 22.Tap dancing 23.c 24.b 25.c)Windy and f)Lanky 26.False 27.b 28.c 29.d 30.True 31.a

Food and Drink

1.b 2.b 3.a 4.True – it can only be made in Derbyshire, Leicestershire and Nottinghamshire. 5.c 6.a 7.Either 8.j 9.b 10.True 11.a 12.a 13.a 14.*M*A*S*H* 15.b 16.b 17.a 18.b 19.a 20.True 21.a 22.c 23.a 24.b 25.False 26.a

Sport

1.c 2.Indianapolis 3.a 4.a 5.False – it is the home of Harlequins Rugby Club. 6.a 7.Both 8.c 9.False 10.a 11.b 12.a 13.c 14.c 15.True 16.b 17.c 18.b 19.True 20.a 21.a – it is slang for a fastball that is especially hard to hit and therefore appears no bigger than a small tablet. 22.a 23.a 24.Rugby union 25.c 26.False 27.a 28.a

Geography

1.Kyrgyzstan 2.a 3.False 4.b 5.Interpol 6.a 7.c 8.c 9.The Marseillaise 10.b 11.c 12.True 13.b 14.a 15.c 16.False 17.b 18.Cork 19.b 20.c 21.b 22.c 23.b

Words

1.a – but b is equally correct. 2.b 3.Tooth 4.He meant 'eligible'. 5.c 6.False 7.b 8.a 9.He meant 'recently deceased'. 10.Mullet 11.c 12.Long 13.b 14.a 15.Bees 16.b 17.Donald 18.b 19.a 20.a 21.c 22.He should have said 'affluent society'. 23.c

SECTION 5

History

1.a 2.b 3.True 4.a 5.a 6.False 7.a 8.a 9.b 10.a 11.a 12.St Valentine's 13.b 14.c 15.False 16.b 17.c 18.b 19.a 20.b 21.False – it was Herbert Hoover; Henry Hoover is a vacuum cleaner. 22.a 23.a 24.b

Science and Nature

1.a 2.c 3.False 4.b 5.b 6.b 7.False – Def Leppard is a UK heavy metal band. 8.c 9.c 10.c 11.False 12.b 13.Ants 14.c 15.False 16.b 17.A hippopotamus 18.c 19.False 20.a 21.c 22.False 23.z 24.a, and possibly c

Maths

1.Child C, partly for being uncaring and partly for being an investment banker, which amounts to much the same thing. 2.None, it's a hole. 3.Three 4.c 5.c 6.False – it is something you learn in maths at school and never need again for the rest of your life. 7.Twenty 8.Any time after 11.

The Arts

1.a 2.b 3.Bill Clinton 4.b 5.a, b and d 6.c 7.False 8.a 9.c 10.a 11.b 12.f 13.a 14.False 15.b 16.c 17.c 18.c 19.a 20.False 21.b 22.c 23.b 24.c 25.True 26.c – although its presence might have hastened Mr Darcy's exit from the lake. 27.a 28.c 29.c – best to be on the safe side.

Food and Drink

1.c 2.False 3.b 4.a 5.b 6.c 7.False 8.d 9.Try eggs. 10.a
11.a and b 12.a 13.c 14.False 15.c 16.a 17.a 18.c 19.False
– surprisingly, it was named after the city's Waldorf
Hotel. 20.a 21.b 22.a 23.c – after Russian ballerina Anna
Pavlova. 24.c

Sport

1.a 2.c 3.Four men in a bobsleigh. 4.a 5.c 6.False 7.a
8.a, b and c 9.a 10.a 11.c 12.False – a rest is the name of
the stick on which pool players place their cue stick in
order to reach the cue ball when it is more than an arm's
length away. 13.a 14.a 15.a 16.b 17.False 18.a 19.c 20.a 21.c
22.b 23.a 24.False 25.a 26.a

Geography

1.a 2.South Island – you knew you could do it! 3.b 4.c
5.c 6.c 7.a 8.a 9.c 10.False 11.c 12.b 13.a – after Charles
Darwin. 14.a 15.She had a kimono draggin' as opposed
to a large lizard. 16.c 17.b 18.c 19.False 20.c 21.b 22.a 23.a
24.c 25.c

Words

1.a 2.On 3.c 4.He meant the gravy train. 5.False 6.b
7.Burnt to the ground. 8.a 9.four 10.'Go Dutch' means
they would split the bill. 11.a 12.c – you can beat an egg,
you can beat a carpet, but you can't beat a nice cup of
tea. 13.a 14.c 15.Instant photographs 16.b 17.Genuine 18.A
wolf in sheep's clothing 19.Something that is unlawful
20.a 21.b – it is a sweet pastry filled with chopped nuts
and honey. 22.Brasserie 23.a 24.He meant a Lazy Boy
recliner. 25.a 26.a 27.Rudolph

Now for the moment of reckoning. Can you hold your head up high or is it time you were quietly put out to graze?

With one point for every correct answer, there are a possible **1,040 points** in total. Here is how your score ranks:

800–1,090: Congratulations! Your levels of grey matter are impressively high.

500–800: A commendable effort, but don't rush to audition for any TV quiz shows just yet.

100–500: It is acceptable to be ignorant in some areas, but you have abused the privilege.

0–100: Did you lend your brain to a neighbour and forget to ask for it back?